Living Waters

Selected Sermons by
Rabbi Elliot J. Cosgrove

Living Waters

Selected Sermons by
Rabbi Elliot J. Cosgrove

2013–2014 / 5774

ParkAvenue Synagogue ק"ק אגודת ישרים

Living Waters: Selected Sermons by Rabbi Elliot J. Cosgrove
2013–2014 / 5774

ParkAvenue
Synagogue ק"ק אגודת ישרים

ISBN 978-0-989-767-2-2-4

Printed in the United States of America in 2014

Park Avenue Synagogue
50 East 87th Street
New York, NY 10128
www.pasyn.org

Contents

Foreword

The conversation that Jews have about how to live and what is right began when God revealed the Ten Commandments to Moses on Mount Sinai. That conversation has continued wherever there were Jews. Even when we were driven from our homeland and scattered over the world, the Jewish people kept that conversation alive through learning and discussion about life and Torah. Today at Park Avenue Synagogue that conversation is as vibrant and relevant as it has ever been. Week after week, Rabbi Cosgrove generates thoughtful, inspiring sermons, connecting the lessons of the parashah to modernity and to our community. The sermons collected in this volume are the latest installments in our ongoing conversation. They break new ground and advance the discussion about our most important task: to observe the Jewish religion and to lead good and moral lives.

As a new Chairman, I am continually impressed by both the quantity and the quality of our rabbi's sermons. The body of work these sermons have made up over Rabbi Cosgrove's six years at Park Avenue Synagogue is impressive by anyone's standards. I would like to thank our past Chairman Steve Friedman for the inspired decision to publish annual sermon collections. Six years ago, it was an innovation; today, it is a tradition. This sixth volume of sermons is entitled "Living Waters," a phrase taken from Genesis 26:19, in the sixth parashah in the Torah, when Isaac is digging wells in the desert.

"Living Waters" are waters from a natural source such as rainwater or water from a spring, ocean or lake, which sustain life. A well-constructed sermon, which brings to life and makes relevant our ancient Torah, is like living water in that it sustains and reinvigorates our lives as Jews today.

In his preface to the first sermon volume, *In the Beginning*, Rabbi Cosgrove wrote: "Every time I preach, I am driven by a single goal – to communicate the ongoing relevance of Judaism to the contemporary Jew." In his sixth year, Rabbi Cosgrove has achieved that goal and reached new heights. The collection of sermons you hold in your hands shows a rabbi in touch with all of the major issues facing twenty-first century American Jews.

In his Rosh Hashanah sermon "Return," Rabbi Cosgrove outlined the mission of Park Avenue Synagogue to create a compelling model of Jewish living that will meet American Jews where they are and provide a path for return. In recent years we have consciously moved to "meet people where they are" and bring them into the community by creating multiple portals of engagement that are responsive to their lives today. The vibrancy of our community reflects that.

In "Radical Hospitality," directly addressing this year's Pew Research Report, Rabbi Cosgrove uses the example of Abraham who would "welcome everyone, invest in everyone, greet everyone, make everyone feel that their presence matters." These are certainly inspiring words for our membership committee, and also for every member of the community.

In one of his most important sermons of the year, the rabbi asked, "Why Synagogue?" In an era when people can purchase access to Jewish ritual and education à la carte, what unique role does a synagogue play? Rabbi Cosgrove argues that a synagogue's role is to be a place where people may experience God's presence, as individuals and together as a community. He adds that a synagogue is the only institution that fulfills its mission by being part of a person's life literally from cradle to grave.

The relationship between God, the Jewish people, Moses and Aaron gave Rabbi Cosgrove a backdrop to comment on the balance of individual accomplishment and institutional imperative. In "It's Not About You," the rabbi points out that while great leaders are important to any community, ultimately the mission and principles take priority over any individual.

Recognizing the historic bat mitzvah of Mordecai Kaplan's daughter in 1922, Rabbi Cosgrove explores ritual change in "On Ritual Innovation." His goal is "to create a service of the mind and heart, responsive to those sitting in the pews and accessible to those seeking a point of entry."

In "Doing Jewish With Other Jews," the rabbi explores how social connectivity and community can build Jewish identity, putting forth the proposition that Jewish identity and connection to Jewish community depend not necessarily on what you believe, but on what you do and with whom.

Towards the end of the year, in "What We Talk About When We Talk About Conversion," Rabbi Cosgrove picked up on an innovative idea that he had introduced in a sermon last year regarding the Jewish community's approach to conversion. It is a proposal that, while committed to Jews marrying Jews and creating Jewish homes, encourages and welcomes people to join the Jewish community.

While these sermons are wonderful to read, they are even more inspiring to hear live in the synagogue. Every week our clergy team engages us with thought-provoking sermons together with inspiring prayer and beautiful music. Park Avenue Synagogue's eclectic blend of tradition and innovation provides "living waters" to sustain and address the needs of our community as they evolve. I hope you to see you on Shabbat.

L'shalom,
Art Penn
Chairman of the Board

Preface

> *Isaac dug anew the wells which had been dug in the days of his fa-*
> *ther Abraham and which the Philistines had stopped up after*
> *Abraham's death. He gave them the same names that his father*
> *had given them. Isaac's servants dug in the wadi and found there*
> *a well of **Living Waters**.* —Genesis 26:18-19

Unlike his father Abraham, Isaac had to find his faith without the benefit of a personal call from God. Estranged from his half-brother Ishmael, bound on the altar as a child, and left bereft following the death of his mother Sarah, Isaac's ability to lead the next Jewish generation was far from guaranteed. Isaac's courageous decision to re-dig his father's wells stands as the first act of Jewish continuity on record.

Ever since, the secret to Jewish vitality has rested on the ability of one generation to draw upon the efforts of prior generations. We draw our life-giving waters of Torah from the same wells as those who preceded us, and so too, we ensure there will be wells for the next generation. Should the wells dry up, we re-dig, and on occasion, we may even dig new ones. Our commitments to God, Torah, and Israel remain as strong as they did in days of old.

As I prepare my sermons for our community, the image of Isaac re-digging his father's wells often comes to mind. I am neither the first nor the last to speak on any weekly portion. Whether it was my own grandfather of blessed memory, or any one of the thousands of preachers of generations past, I know that I stand on the shoulders of giants. Unlike other genres of expression, originality of thought is not necessarily the guiding criterion for a successful sermon. A good sermon draws on the insights of the teachers who came before. A good rabbi understands the function of a sermon as transmitting tradition anew to the community he or she serves. A sermon must have a feeling of relevance and urgency, but it must evince a sense of being anchored in the past and invested in the future. The waters I draw from are living, but the wells are not new. I am humbled to be one link in a sacred chain of transmission.

Not only sermons, but the mission of Park Avenue Synagogue also falls squarely within the guiding metaphor of this volume's title. What is a dynamic synagogue if not an institutional opportunity to bring the values, practices, and faith of our people into relief for a new generation? Our present success is drawn from the insistence of our lay and professional leadership on bringing creativity, vigor, and excellence to everything we do. As a transmitter of personal and communal identity, our synagogue is a vehicle of both conservation and change. We are not merely guardians of the Jewish past. We seek to project our faith in a voice that is meaningful to present and future generations.

I am grateful to the Board and Officers of Park Avenue Synagogue for their trust and confidence in me and my professional colleagues. Our enthusiasm is wrought from the passion of our membership. The synergistic relationship between Jewish educators and committed lay leaders makes us who we are. Art Penn, I congratulate you on completing your first year as Chairman. Your tireless energy, boundless good will, and belief in the mission of our synagogue are an inspiration to us all. I look forward to years of partnership and friendship with you and your extraordinary team of lay leaders.

Thank you to my colleague Marga Hirsch for your ongoing and masterful editing and for overseeing the publication of this sermon collection. Many thanks to Jean Bloch Rosensaft and to Rebecca Raphael Feuerstein for your careful input in the preparation of this volume.

I have been blessed with many teachers in my life and I am grateful to them all. First among equals is my doctoral advisor at the University of Chicago, Professor Paul Mendes-Flohr. Professor Mendes-Flohr is a living exemplar of a "scholar-gentleman," embodying the ideals of critical analysis, clarity of expression, intellectual rigor, and steadfast kindness. At a critical stage of my life, Professor Mendes-Flohr intervened and set the course for my intellectual and professional journey. I will be forever grateful for his intellectual mentorship, for the model of his *menschlichkeit*, and most of all, for believing in me. It is a badge of honor to be one of "Paul's students," and it is to him that I dedicate this book.

Elliot J. Cosgrove
July 21, 2014
23 *Tammuz* 5774

Erev Rosh Hashanah

Favorable Judgment

Goldstein, after much delay and against his better judgment, finally gave in and agreed to go on a camping trip with his dear friend Cohen. At the end of the first day, exhausted, they set up camp, ready for a night under the stars. At that very moment, they hear a growl coming from the woods, the leaves rustle, and not more than ten feet away, they see the outline of a very big, very angry, and very scary black bear. Without missing a beat, Goldstein reaches over, grabs his sneakers, and starts lacing them up. Cohen sees what his friend is up to and whispers, "Goldstein! What are you doing? You can't possibly outrun the bear." Goldstein turns to his companion and says, "Cohen, I don't need to outrun the bear, I just need to outrun you!"

Shanah Tovah! On behalf of Cantor Schwartz, Rabbi Rein, Cantor Lissek – the newest member of the PAS clergy team – our new Chairman Art Penn, the leadership of Park Avenue Synagogue, Goldstein, on behalf of all of us, I wish you, your families, the people Israel, and all of humanity, a sweet, happy and health-filled new year.

I hope, at this moment, everyone feels good. Because truth be told, if the cantor and I do our job well over the next ten days, that feeling won't last very long. Like the story of the Garden of Eden, the progression of these holidays reflects the promises and pitfalls of what it means to be human. On Rosh Hashanah we recall not only the creation of the world, but of the first human being, made in God's image, endowed with unlimited freedom, beholding the miracle of creation.

And then, without pause, we are reminded of how we have abused those freedoms, given in to temptation, and fallen short of the potential of our promise. Over the next ten days we will recount our sins and perform painful inventories of the soul, all with the aim of doing *teshuvah*, returning to being the people we thought we could be. Not all wrongs can be righted and not all that is crooked can be made straight. But the spiritual itinerary of these holidays is to traverse our humanity from its heights to its depths and then back again. In doing so, we seek to enter the coming year wiser and more hopeful.

This year, this evening, on this Day of Judgment, I want to take our examination of the flawed nature of the human condition in a slightly different and perhaps unexpected direction. To observe that the holidays are meant to remind us that we have all sinned in the year gone by is an insight that is neither new nor interesting. "We are not so arrogant," the *mahzor* teaches, "as to say before you our God that we are righteous and have not sinned for we have sinned." We acknowledge the wrongs we have committed – in public and in private, knowingly and unknowingly, against God and our fellow man – in alphabetical acrostics, fist on chest, one after another, covering the full range of human failing. Ten days from now, just before we chant *Kol Nidrei*, we will ask for permission to pray with the sinners, which, if you stop to think about it, is a liturgical sleight of hand to drill down that you and I, each one of us, is included in that very category. Today reminds us of what Ecclesiastes knew long ago: "There is not a righteous man upon earth who does good and sins not." (7:20)

But tonight I want to go even further, because I believe that this process of self-reflection, *heshbon ha-nefesh*, of "moral inventory-ing" is only half the story. After all, some of us may arrive here tonight aware of our faults. I hope most of us are open to the possibility that in the days ahead we may discover in ourselves a fault or two. But I am willing to bet that all of us came here able to point out the faults of our family, friends, and others, who we believe, in the year gone by, have what to atone for. Remember the story of Goldstein and Cohen, sworn enemies (they meet again), who see each other as they are walking out of shul on Rosh Hashanah. Cohen decides that this year he is going to take the high ground and greets Goldstein with a big hug and a smile: "Goldstein, tonight I prayed for you. I prayed everything for you that

you prayed for me." To which Goldstein replies: "*Nu* . . . are you start-
ing with me already?" Tonight, we know our task is not just about self-
reflection, but also about granting forgiveness to others, even those
people – especially those people – whom we would be otherwise dis-
inclined to forgive.

All of which, of course, begs the uncomfortable but unavoidable
question: How does recognizing our own faults affect our ability to
judge those whom we believe to have sinned in the year gone by? Does
an awareness of our own shortcomings have implications for our ability to redress, resolve, and reconcile with others? Dressed in our holiday finest, we are tempted to proclaim our righteousness, to see
ourselves as of unimpeachable moral quality. Not so, says the *Maḥzor*.
By focusing on our own flaws, the holidays ensure that we do not un-
duly skew our righteousness about that of others. As the Hasidic Rabbi
Wolf of Strikov taught: "Remember that you are not as good as you
think you are, and the world is not as bad as you think it is." (Cited in
Rabbi Joseph Telushkin, *A Code of Jewish Ethics*, v.1, p. 83)

In his book on ethics, my colleague and teacher Rabbi Joseph
Telushkin explains that we all invariably judge other people according
to a standard which we could never live up to ourselves. We are quick
to provide context and rationalizations for our own misdeeds, but never
think to grant that same courtesy to others. We bend and twist the
moral arc of the universe to conform to our own sensibilities, as if any
of us could possibly be objective about judging ourselves. What is
more, our very reluctance to be candid about our own sins inevitably
distorts our assessment of others. Long before Freud identified the
psychological defense mechanism of "projection," there has always
been a human tendency to see in others those very traits we deny having personally. As the Hasidic master the Baal Shem Tov wrote, "The
world is a mirror. Inasmuch as a person is blind to one's own faults,
God arranged it to see them in other people. The defects you see in
others are your own." (Cited in Rabbi Abraham J. Twerski, *A Formula
for Proper Living*, p. 62) Consider the troubling scene in tomorrow's
haftorah when the High Priest Eli callously reproaches the weeping
and prayerful Hannah, accusing her of being drunk. None of us ever
knows the whole truth, and yet again and again in the past year, we
have rendered judgment, proclaimed ourselves judge, jury, and sen-

tencing agent to countless people, denying them the very due process that we would want for ourselves. The power of these holidays is that they call on us to entertain the inconvenient possibility that we would rather avoid when confronting our loved ones with their faults: namely, that you and I, all of us, are terribly flawed, altogether defective, and far more accountable for the deficiencies of our imperfect world than we would like to let on.

Unlike Christians, as Jews we do not believe that we are born sinful, nor, at the opposite end, to use Reinhold Niebuhr's language, that we are "moral men in an immoral society." As Jews we believe ourselves to be creations of mixed morality in a society chock-full of temptation. From the Garden of Eden onward, we have been endowed with both a good and an evil inclination. And as God counsels Cain just before he slays his brother Abel, the evil inclination crouches in wait. Its urge is towards us, but we can, if we try hard, master it. Some of us do, and some of us don't, but the struggle is neverending for us all. All of which means that for Jews the difference between a moral and immoral person is not whether she or he possesses the capacity for wrongdoing; the difference is whether she or he demonstrates the ability to restrain the inclination which we all equally possess. I am fond of quoting the pre-wedding advice of my Granny of blessed memory: "Elliot, you can get your appetite anywhere you want, just make sure you eat at home." None of us dare be too assured in our self-righteousness, as we are all made of flesh and blood. We may not all live in glass houses, but we all put our pants on one leg at a time. Lace up as fast as you can, but these holidays are here to tell you that the difference – the distance – between you and the person about whom you sit in judgment is not as large as you think.

Which brings us back to the central question. If indeed all of us are flawed, and if indeed we know that the flaws we see in others are very possibly projections of our own shortcomings, or by definition, possibilities rooted in our own humanity, then how exactly does one go about judging others? If the playing field of the human condition is flatter than we think, is there such a thing as a moral high ground?

To begin with, and to state the obvious, one answer is not: "Not to judge." We do not live in a world of moral relativism. There is a right and there is a wrong and there are many people who have crossed the line. From the moment we ate of the fruit, we were granted the ability to distinguish between good and evil, which means that a person is always accountable for his or her behavior. According to Jewish law, *Adam mued l'olam*, "A person is always responsible." To confess our own sins, to know ourselves to be human in no way exempts others from culpability.

But what it does mean is that the measure of our judgment is to be reckoned not just in terms of the application of justice, but in its being guided by a sense of modesty and humility. Do we know all the facts of the case, or is our judgment based only on hearsay? As Rabbi Telushkin notes, even when God was set to destroy Sodom and Gomorrah for their wickedness, God went down to see things firsthand. (p. 76) Not every conversation this week needs to begin with accusations. There is nothing wrong, in fact there is everything right, with beginning a difficult conversation by acknowledging that you have only one side – your side – of the story. Don't be so quick to rush to judgment; ask for the facts first. And if you should discover that in the past year you have unfairly suspected your neighbor of a misdeed, the Talmud explains, that person must be pacified and blessed. (Berachot 31b, Jerusalem Talmud 93). We must be modest in judgment if for no other than because that is the basic decency we would ask of others regarding our own actions.

Next, in acknowledging our own flawed humanity, we may also find that it is often, but not necessarily, the case that it is our own actions that have led to a relationship being in disrepair. It is far too easy to point out how we have been wronged, how others have let us down. They started it, they should be the one to call, it is on them to make amends. Really? Is it ever really so simple? I doubt it. Anyone familiar with the twelve-step program knows the pivotal importance of the fourth step – taking a moral inventory. Why? Because such an accounting illuminates how each of us bears responsibility for the condition of the relationships most dear to us. In the days ahead we must be willing to stand face-to-face with our own failings in order that we may ask how we are responsible for the broken relationships of our lives.

And yes, while nobody in this world gets a free pass, in the days ahead, as the lens of our concern extends far and wide, it is incumbent upon us to consider how society itself bears corporate responsibility for individual wrongs. A story is told of Fiorello La Guardia; prior to becoming mayor, he was presiding one evening in night court. The defendant was an impoverished woman charged with stealing a loaf of bread to feed her family. Despite La Guardia's request, the shopkeeper refused to drop the charges – a lesson must be taught, an example must be made, such behavior must not be tolerated. The law was the law, and La Guardia laid down the punishment: ten dollars or ten days in jail. Then he took ten dollars from his pocket, put it in a hat and announced that everyone in the room be fined fifty cents for living in a town where a person has to steal a loaf of bread to feed her family. According to the next day's paper, $47.50 was collected and given to the accused – including 50 cents from the aggrieved shopkeeper himself. If nothing else, the point of these holidays is to communicate that we are all stewards of God's creation; every one of us is responsible for the imperfect world in which we live. Acknowledging our own failings doesn't mitigate the sins of others, but it does highlight that our moral posture is not to be measured only by our ability to feel righteous indignation. Our moral posture is measured by whether we have leveraged that indignation towards establishing a world filled with righteousness.

Finally, an abiding awareness of our sins, quotidian and otherwise, demands that we judge others with empathy, in the words of *Pirkei Avot*: "Judge every person favorably." (1:6) We would all do well to imitate the attitude of the eighteenth-century Hasidic Rabbi Elimelech of Lizensk, who would begin his prayers: "May I see the good traits of others and not their defects." (Telushkin, p. 75). We should do so because it could turn out that our allegations are mistaken. We should do so because it is far more pleasant to go through life believing in a humanity that is fundamentally good and not bad. We should do so because the other person, wrong as he or she may be, is still a human being created in God's image. We should do so because there is not one of us here who does not have a past. I know that I personally would never want the totality of my being judged on the basis of one misdeed. None of us can or should be reduced to a single incident – good or bad. The message of these holidays is that all of us are capable of growth. The past must not be wielded like a stick to be used by the present to blemish someone's future. But most of all, we need to judge others with empathy because this is exactly what we are here to ask God to do for us. The Talmud explains that it is the person who is *ma'avir al midotav*, able to overlook the shortcomings of his fellow, who will accordingly be judged favorably by God (Babylonian Talmud, Shabbat 127b). Tomorrow we will beg of God, *L'khol p'sha'im tekhaseh b'ahavah*, "Cover our sins with love." God help us all if we prove incapable of extending to others the opportunity to grow and begin anew. We can, if we so choose, be God-like in the attribute of mercy. Today can be the day we flip the calendar and rewrite the narrative, not just for ourselves, but for everyone looking to make a new start.

The midrash tells of Rabbi Yossi ben Halafta who was once asked by a Roman matron to explain what exactly God has been doing since the six days of creation. It is a timely question, certainly this evening, marking the anniversary of that very creation. Rabbi Yossi replied that ever since that first week, God has been building ladders: Some ladders for people to ascend and other ladders for people to descend. (Leviticus Rabbah 8:1)

Friends, I don't know where you stand on your ladder, and whether you have ascended or descended in the year gone by – that is something for you to reflect on in the days ahead. What I do know is that no matter which rung you are on, right now we are all just trying our darndest to pull ourselves up a little higher. Perhaps this year, in recognizing that very struggle which is our own, we can also be a little God-like, stop trying to outrun our humanity and instead give a boost to another soul similarly struggling to climb. It is not a zero-sum game. There is more than enough forgiveness to go around and, God knows, we all need all the help we can get. *L'elah u-l'elah*, higher and higher let us climb, and with each other's help we will greet this New Year in health, happiness, forgiveness, and peace.

Rosh Hashanah

Return

Franz Rosenzweig's decision to attend Rosh Hashanah services exactly one hundred years ago today, oddly, came down to a procedural matter. The only son of a wealthy industrialist, Rosenzweig belonged to a generation of German Jewry fully integrated into the social, cultural, and material opportunities of the time. His Judaism, lacking in depth and devotion, simply could not compete with his passions for music and for Goethe or with his professional aspirations – first a medical degree and then, turning to philosophy, a doctoral thesis on Hegel. His cousin had converted to Christianity, as had his best friend and intellectual sparring partner Eugen Rosenstock. Over time, Judaism's hold on Rosenzweig became increasingly tenuous. Finally, in the summer of 1913, after an all-night conversation with Rosenstock, Rosenzweig made the fateful decision to convert to Christianity. But because he was a philosopher with too much time on his hands, he wanted his conversion to be as kosher as possible – mirroring the journey of the New Testament Paul who became a Christian by way of Judaism. For Rosenzweig, that meant going to Rosh Hashanah services back home in Kassel. The post-services scene is related in Nahum Glatzer's volume on Rosenzweig's life. "Mother," Franz explained, "here is everything, here is the truth. There is only one way, Jesus." His mother, Adele, confused and I imagine somewhat irritated, inquired: "Were you not in synagogue on New Year's Day?" "Yes," Franz replied, "and I will go to the synagogue on the Day of Atonement, too. I am still a Jew." At which point Adele told her son that she was contacting the synagogue to make sure that he not be allowed in: "In our Synagogue," she said, "there is no room for an apostate." (*Franz Rosenzweig: His Life and Thought*, p. 25)

Oh, to be a fly on the wall in the Rosenzweig household! Not surprisingly, young Franz did not stay in Kassel that Yom Kippur. He left for Berlin and found a seat in the synagogue led by Rabbi Markus Petuchowski. Nobody knows exactly what took place during services that day. Rosenzweig never spoke of it openly nor did he ever write about it. What we do know is that Rosenzweig left those services a changed man, informing his friends a few days later: "I shall remain a Jew." What had been intended as a final Jewish pit stop on the road to Christianity became a first step back into Jewish life. But as many of you may know, Rosenzweig's spiritual odyssey was not only a personal one. On the back of postcards, literally from the trenches of World War I, he wrote his book *The Star of Redemption*, a momentous contribution to modern Jewish thought. He turned down a prestigious university post, turning his energies towards revitalizing German Jewish life. In 1920 he founded the *Lehrhaus*, a center of Jewish learning in Frankfurt, whose institutional mission was to facilitate the journey of assimilated German Jews, as he himself once was, back into their ancestral patrimony. The force of Rosenzweig's vision, his flair for public relations and "big lectures," assembling a veritable who's who of intellectual muscle – Buber, Nobel, Oppenheimer, Scholem, Agnon, among others – created a magical atmosphere of learning; the *Lehrhaus* drew hundreds of Jews enthusiastically returning to the heritage from which they were estranged.

Rosenzweig would not live to realize the fullness of his vision. Stricken with ALS in 1922, he endured a debilitating seven-year struggle until his tragic early passing in 1929 at the age of 43. His vision for a revitalized German Jewry, we know, would be cut down with the rise of Hitler just a few years later. "The pity of it all," to borrow Amos Elon's words: a would-be renaissance stopped in its tracks, an inspired vision of return never fulfilled.

When we enter the synagogue on the High Holidays, we are on a journey of return. There is no exact English word for *teshuvah*, often translated as "repentance" or "remorse," but it is perhaps best explained as "return" or "homecoming." Which is, of course, precisely the sentiment we should be filled with at this moment. We have returned to this sacred space, this holy moment on the Jewish calendar, knowing we have been away too long. The melodies, the foods, the faces, the traditions – in the year gone by we have grown distant from our heritage and on these holidays we seek to return to a warm embrace. But we know, as Rosenzweig himself came to discover, that the return is also one of far deeper significance. Today, we ask for one thing, *ahat sha'alti*, to return to our best selves, to our former selves, and to our God. Unhitched from our moorings, we have been spiritually displaced long enough, and today we begin the journey home.

One hundred years after Rosenzweig's momentous homecoming, I believe that his vision remains just as – if not more – instructive, inspiring, and applicable to us today as it did to his community then. On this day when we gather as a Jewish community to articulate our path forward, if I could distill our mission into a single word, it would be what Rosenzweig discovered, and that is: "Return." Not just today, but every day of the year: to facilitate the return of an alienated American Jewry back to the Jewish tradition, God, and peoplehood that is their rightful heritage to claim. Those of you with a scorecard may recall the very first sentence I spoke to you when I was installed as your rabbi: *Hashiveinu Hashem elekha v'nashuva. Hadesh yameinu k'kedem*, "Return us Lord unto You, and we shall return. Renew our days, as in days of old." (Lamentations 5:21) The song, as it goes, remains the same, but the urgency and conviction with which we must embrace this mission has never been greater. The time is now. With deep humility, with profound love and concern for the Jewish people, as your Rabbi, I call for a bold paradigm shift in how we define our mission. Today – *hayom* – as this holy day instructs, we must be willing to break with the past. We must be attentive to the present – *hineni* – and most importantly, we must be willing to imagine new worlds of possibility for the future.

This year not only marks one hundred years since Rosenzweig's decision to return to Judaism, it is also one hundred years since Solomon Schechter founded the United Synagogue of Conservative Judaism, of which Park Avenue is a card-carrying, dues-paying member. Schechter, the head of the Jewish Theological Seminary, understood the tectonic shifts taking place in American Jewry between 1880 and 1920 as millions of Russian and Eastern European Jews arrived on American shores. The ideology of the Conservative movement, the educational vision of JTS, the blossoming of the United Synagogue, all reflected the arrival of an immigrant population to its new environment – not just geographically, but culturally, linguistically, economically, and otherwise. As Schechter himself put it: "In order to be a success in the American rabbinate, you must be able to talk baseball." Schechter's brilliance was that he created a movement, ideologically and institutionally, that was right for its moment. What are the great Conservative synagogues of Great Neck, Shaker Heights, Pikesville, and Paterson if not the communal structures by which an upwardly mobile American Jewry reconstituted itself in suburbia? What is the Conservative movement's signature focus on the tension between scholarship and faith if not a window into an old world/new world, Chaim Potok-esque experience of the children of a yeshiva-trained generation receiving a secular education? Whether we do or do not introduce instrumental music into our services, whether you can or can't drive to synagogue on Shabbat, is swordfish kosher or isn't it? Every one of these conversations and a million others reflect a movement that emerged in response to a specific set of historical and sociological circumstances. In the words of the famed observer of American Jewry, Marshall Sklare, " . . . the signal contribution of Conservatism would seem to be that of offering an acceptable pattern of adjustment to the American environment for many East European-derived Jews." (*Conservative Judaism: An American Religious Movement*, p. 249)

I am not supposed to pick favorite congregants, but if I did, it would be my oldest – Irene Eisenberg. At 102, you should live to 120! Every time I visit Mrs. Eisenberg, after she has offered me a drink, and after she shows me the letter from President Obama wishing her a happy 100th, after she shares that she still worries for her children – all now in their late seventies with grandchildren of their own, she always tells me the same story. It is the story of how she and her late husband Alex – both products of Orchard Street on the Lower East Side – fell in love. They couldn't afford a honeymoon, so they took a carriage ride on their wedding day and went all the way up to Fifth Avenue. On that day, Irene turned to her groom and said, "Someday my love, we are going to live on this street." And every time she tells me this story – as we sip our soda and look out her window onto Central Park – in all the emotion, I am struck by the journey of American Jewry. From the Lower to the Upper East Side, or from the Bronx, or Brooklyn, direct or by way of Riverdale, Scarsdale, or Farmingdale, it is a journey that one hundred years ago, Schechter prepared for, a journey that today, Irene knows, we know, has found fulfillment.

Schechter and Rosenzweig were prophetic leaders. Their visions are not in competition; neither one is better nor worse. We remember them both because they did the very thing that visionary Jewish leadership does in every generation, the same thing that we must do today. Namely, ask the question: Given the condition of contemporary Jewry, what is the ideological and institutional path that will best ensure a vital Jewish future? One hundred years later, I can say with absolute surety that the immigrant experience to which Schechter responded is no longer our own, but Rosenzweig's program of return is altogether resonant. The differences between Rosenzweig's Germany and our America are as profound as they are numerous, but his assumptions about the Jewry of his day and his spirited efforts to win back a secularized community are instructive for us. According to my teacher Paul Mendes-Flohr, Rosenzweig's gift was that he "neither condemned nor stigmatized the alienation from Judaism of the acculturated Jew – indeed, in some sense he even honored it." (*German-Jewish History in Modern Times*, ed. Michael Meyer, v. 4, p. 140) He understood the alienation of the modern Jew – after all, it was once his own – and he provided the tools by which the Jews of his time could return home. And so too, must we today. The educational mission of this and like-minded congregations must be to create a dynamic, authentic, and compelling model of Jewish life and living that will meet the searching American Jew where she or he is, and provide the path for return.

I promise you, the return of the contemporary Jew standing at the periphery of Jewish life is not contingent on whether swordfish is or isn't kosher, under which circumstances it is or isn't permissible to drive on Shabbat, and who did or didn't write the Torah. If we want an American Jewish renaissance to occur, we need to explain the power of *kashrut*, the sanctity of the Sabbath, and the thrill of reading a sacred text that, though written long ago, speaks to our souls with an unnerving intimacy. We need to spend less time debating modifications to the prayer book and more time teaching people how to pray. Less time debating who wrote the Bible and more time helping people read the Bible with passion. Rosenzweig envisioned a model of Jewish learning "in reverse order." Meaning Jewish learning that begins not by flinging a page of Talmud in front of a Jew for whom that page has no meaning, but by first seeking to understand the concerns of a secular Jew and then establishing the relevance of our sacred texts as they apply to those very concerns. A Judaism that is both traditional and liberal in its inclinations, unapologetically claiming the mantle of authenticity, but eyes wide open about the condition and leanings of the American Jew. Gone are the days when a synagogue – ours or any other – can assume an insular, parochial, and tradition-bound community. Judaism functions in the marketplace of ideas and consumer choice. We cannot assume that the Jew in the pew, if he or she is in the pew at all, is remotely at home with the language, rituals, and associations of Jewish life and living. I am, nevertheless, entirely optimistic. I do not believe for a second that contemporary Jewry has rejected *Yiddishkeit*. We are just as thirsty for spiritual sustenance, for communities of meaning, for a connection to an everlasting tradition as any generation of Jews. We just do not know how to get our foot in the door and we are stuck in the assumptions of a bygone era. Our synagogue must provide the portals of entry, show the relevance, direct Jews out of their spiritual cul-de-sacs, and mark out the path forward – the path of return.

If there is one message of the High Holidays, it is that before we change the world, we need to change ourselves, or as the book title goes, "Foreign Policy Begins at Home." (Richard N. Haass, 2014) The best form of leadership our shul can provide is not to tell people how they should conduct themselves, not to tell the Conservative movement how to recast its mission, but to model something worthy of emulation, to become a laboratory of Jewish life and living from which ideas emerge that will ripple well beyond the four walls of our synagogue. Everything we do should be aimed at facilitating the return of American Jewry to its Judaism, a mission that begins right now.

Why is The Park Avenue Synagogue Lecture Series this year not on Israel, anti-Semitism, or the landscape of American Jewry, but on living a meaningful life? Because I want our congregants and would-be congregants to know that our tradition has something to say about ethics, about aging, about addiction, about love and laughter, about all the things you and I go to sleep and wake up thinking about. Our tradition will, if we let it, speak with a relevance and urgency to our searching souls.

Why is the congregational school in the midst of an evolving process of reinventing itself? Because the idea that our children can just be dropped off between 4:00 and 6:00 on a Tuesday afternoon and emerge with a literate and loving relationship to Jewish life is an idea that arose in a different time and place. We must continue working towards a model of Jewish education that sees the Jewish learner not just as the student but as the entire family, a model of education that is experiential, experimental, and all-embracing. Technology has given us incredible tools with which a family can learn to recite *kiddush* at home, say blessings, or study the weekly Torah portion. The cantor's new family *siddur* and CD is but one step in a far grander vision of transforming how and to whom Jewish educational content is delivered. We need to see our learners, as Rosenzweig understood, not merely as children (*banayikh*) – passive recipients of tradition – but as builders (*bonayikh*) – builders of a knowing, believing, doing, and belonging Jewish future.

Why are we spearheading an Upper East Side Hebrew language program this year? The great poet Hayim Nahman Bialik once remarked that "Reading the Bible in translation is like kissing your new bride through a veil." Hebrew literacy is the gateway to Jewish life, to our heritage, to world Jewry, and to our present commitments to Israel. It means you can open up a prayer book, a Bible, an Israeli website and you are a stakeholder in that conversation. I can think of no better personal educational resolution for you to make this year than committing one night a week to the study of Hebrew.

And while I am getting it all out, why will we continue to push the envelope on embracing the non-Jew in our Jewish family? Because I know, and so do you, that neither you nor I can control who our child sits next to in freshman English, first-year Torts, or the first day on the job. Our community will continue to unapologetically preach the value of endogamy – marrying within the Jewish faith – and we will unrepentantly work to facilitate the journey of would-be Jews into our Jewish family. I am, we are, in the business of creating Jewish homes! Our communal culture must be one that facilitates, celebrates, and supports the establishment of Jewish homes – Jewish by birth or conversion, straight or gay, single or married, with or without children.

Facilitating our return to Judaism is why, in the coming weeks, months, and years, we will transform what happens here on Friday nights and Saturday mornings. Beginning on Friday night October 4 when Henry Kissinger speaks, you will see the start of a new model of a Friday night service. I have the best cantor in the world, I know a thing or two about giving sermons, and as Shabbat morning kiddush goes, ours is pretty good. But we have yet to fundamentally change the culture of what takes place here on Friday nights and Shabbat mornings. We sell ourselves – and even worse, our children – short, if all we do is put in a little more or less music, Torah reading, or egg salad and claim to be a flagship synagogue. I refuse to believe that the outstanding contribution American Jewry has to make to Jewish prayer is the responsive reading. We need to reconsider fundamental assumptions: timing, length, music, content, and context. All of it needs to be assessed and re-assessed, constantly evolving into the decades to come. We need to create a service for the heart and the soul, for you, your children, and grandchildren. The kind of service that were Rosenzweig to walk in, he might just be inclined to stay a while, find his place, and know that unacquainted as he might be with the service, he had come home – and it might just be worth coming back again the next week.

I could go on, and I will, please God, into the years to come, about Israel engagement, social justice, arts and culture, Jewish camping, what a Bar or Bat Mitzvah should look like – all the pathways that give voice to an authentic, accessible and relevant vision of Jewish life. But everything on the list must fall under the umbrella mission of "return." If it doesn't, well, then it is doesn't get to wear the Park Avenue Synagogue label. Like a true laboratory, we will experiment. Some things will work and some won't. But we will forgive, we will learn, we will pick ourselves up and try again, and we will know that we left it all out on the field. We will create a laboratory whose work has implications well beyond these walls. Walls, mind you, that in the coming years will need to expand to house our growing and renewed vision.

But the most important player in making all this happen is not me and not the cantor. The most important player in this whole equation is you. *You* coming to shul, *you* signing up for a class, *you* signing up for our first-ever adult learning retreat next month. *You* serving on a committee, performing an act of *ḥesed*, paying a *shiva* call, visiting someone in need of a hospital or home visit. You looking around today or any day of the year for a new face and welcoming a new congregant into the community. Telling your friends that you look forward to them coming over for Friday night dinner and you will meet them not at your home, but at shul – because that is the way you roll as a Jew. What you choose to do and what you choose not to do matters. Each of these choices signals a gesture of return, your willingness to find your way back. It won't happen all at once and it doesn't have to. When Rosenzweig was once asked if he put on *tefillin*, he famously answered, "Not yet." It is a journey of a lifetime that may take a lifetime, but here today let's at least agree on our trajectory and, more importantly, let's make the commitment to begin the journey.

The rabbis tell of a king, who in a fit of anger sent his son away from his kingdom to live in a foreign land. Years passed, the anger subsided, and the king sent a messenger to his son that he longed for his estranged his son to return. The son sent the messenger back to the king explaining that the hurt remained, the distance was too great, he could not – or would not – make the journey. The king received the message and sent back the following reply: "Return as far as you can, and I will meet you the rest of the way."

Friends, ours is a moment of an American Jewry in need of return. If you will take the step forward, I will, I promise, bring this institution halfway. Together we will demonstrate a model of synagogue life that is authentic, accessible, relevant, engaging, and please God, always evolving. We will create a house of learning, of community, and of prayer. A portal of entry for Jews yearning to return. A place that will meet you where you are and take you to the place you long to be. A place that you knew about all along, but had been away from for far too long, a place called home.

Hashiveinu Hashem elekha v'nashuva. Ḥadesh yameinu k'kedem. "Return us Lord unto You, and we shall return. Renew our days, as in days of old."

Yom Kippur

The Fate That Awaits Us All

O
f all the dark and despairing hours of the Yom Kippur War, rock bottom arrived on day three – Tuesday, October 8, 1973. According to later recollections, it was those twenty-four hours that would be remembered as "a critical, almost hopeless . . . struggle for physical survival." (Abraham Rabinovich, *The Yom Kippur War*, p. 269ff.) Just a few decades after the Shoah – emboldened, mistakenly so, by the victory of 1967 – Israel now stood on the brink of destruction. In the Sinai, in the Golan, a fighting force caught wholly unaware, its leadership flatfooted and demoralized – and a world that so recently proclaimed "never again" was apparently letting it happen again.

Nowhere was this sense of desperation more pronounced than among the soldiers of Fort Purkan along the Suez Canal. Fort Purkan was one of a number of Israeli garrisons stationed along the eastern Suez, part of a chain of fortifications known as the Bar-Lev line, intended to defend Israel against any Egyptian assault. In the first hours of the war, it proved to be wholly inadequate, overrun by an Egyptian army who plowed right through and into the Sinai. Some of the garrisons were destroyed immediately, many soldiers were killed or taken prisoner, some contemplated a Masada-like suicide. The thirty-three soldiers of Fort Purkan remained trapped behind enemy lines, separated from any would-be savior. As military histories have subsequently revealed, in those desperate hours Israel's leadership wrestled with the dreadful prospect of abandoning the men of Fort Purkan to their fate rather than risk even more losses – a prospect more and more likely as the shelling of the attacking Egyptian army grew closer.

Surveying a series of terrible options, Purkan's garrison commander Major Wiesel decided to lead his men on foot through the Egyptian second army. He radioed to the Israeli Brigade Commander on the other side, speaking in code – Yiddish, actually – just in case the Egyptians were listening in. On the other end was General Ariel Sharon, commander of the Southern Front. "You haven't got much of a chance," Sharon said, "we can't come and help you." To which Wiesel insisted, "We are leaving anyway." At nightfall, the thirty-three soldiers set out for a rendezvous point six miles east on the Hamutal Ridge. On the Israeli side, two men – Colonel Amnon Reshef and Lieutenant Colonel Shaul Shalev – volunteered for what could best be described as a suicide mission, manning their two tanks with the hope of rescuing their comrades. As daylight broke, the battle waged fiercely as a vastly outnumbered Reshef and Shalev fought their Egyptian enemies, while the soldiers of Fort Purkan remained pinned down under a relentless Egyptian barrage. Reshef was drawn into a platoon of Egyptian commandos leaving only Shalev to complete the mission at hand. Shalev radioed Wiesel to fire a flare into the air to identity their position. Shalev charged forward in their direction, and reached his comrades' location. Four wounded soldiers were quickly lowered through the tank's turret. As for the remaining twenty-nine . . . well, they grabbed onto whatever piece of tank exterior they could and held on for dear life. Nobody then and nobody since had ever witnessed a spectacle like the sight of Shalev's tank as it approached the Israeli camp. Through an onslaught of artillery, a remarkable image moving through the desert, Shalev's tank, covered by the men of Fort Purkan – not one of them, miraculously, killed on that ride home.

According to Abraham Rabinovich's account of the war, reports of Shalev's heroism brought a surge of much-needed good news through the front lines in a country standing on the precipice of its own destruction: Thirty-three men facing certain death, and one man – Lt. Colonel Shalev – pulling them back from the brink.

If you want to know how Yom Kippur is supposed to make you feel, the near-death experience of Lt. Colonel Shalev and the thirty-three men of Fort Purkan is as good a place as any to start. To go toe-to-toe with death and emerge from that experience alive is what this sacred day is all about. That feeling is especially acute on this, the fortieth anniversary of the Yom Kippur war, the moment when, in the words of the journalist Yossi Klein Halevi, all of Israel was forced to glimpse its collective mortality.

It is a jarring and not altogether comfortable thought, but, if you pause to consider it, the picture that emerges is unmistakable. What is today if not an elaborate ceremony meant to foist upon us the feeling of a near-death experience? We fast, we abstain from sexual intimacy, and traditionally we wear white, even a kittel, representing the simple shroud one wears in death. The recitation of the martyrology service, the Yizkor prayers to recall our loved ones, the death-defying service of the High Priest, Jonah's being swallowed up and then spit out by the whale, the clanging gates of *Neilah* – all of it is a process meant to ritualize the central question of these holidays: "Who will live and who will die?" The late Rabbi Alan Lew once explained that the journey between Rosh Hashanah and Yom Kippur is meant to be, in kabbalistic terms, a *kefitzat ha-derekh*, a compressed or contracted journey. Rosh Hashanah representing birth or creation, and today – Yom Kippur – representing death. (*This Is Real and You Are Completely Unprepared*, p. 214) It is not only that we acknowledge the mortal human condition, rather we are asked today to stare directly into the face of our own death. Like Isaac bound on the altar – a hairsbreadth away, it is our own reflection we see in that glistening blade – we live to tell the tale. That is what today is all about.

Given my line of work, it is rare that I go a single week, if not a single day, without being reminded of the shared and inescapable fate that awaits us all. It strikes me that there are really only two things that can be said about death with absolute surety. First, that it will happen, and second, that we don't know when. "From the dust you come and to the dust you return." (Genesis 3:19) It doesn't matter who you are, death is, if nothing else, democratic. As the Italian proverb goes: "After the game, the king and the pawn go into the same box." And then, of course, there is the mystery of when. From the very beginning, the midrash explains, God concealed the day of death from all of us. Who will live and who will die? None of us knows – that is why it is framed as a question.

As Jews we like to bless each other to live until Moses' ripe old age of 120, but there are no guarantees. You may recall the story of the rabbi making visits at the nursing home just before the holidays. He went to visit Mrs. Cohen, greeted her and asked how old she was.

"Eighty," Mrs. Cohen replied, to which the rabbi appropriately responded: "Mrs. Cohen, may the next forty years be filled with health and happiness." He then walked into Mrs. Schwartz's room. A warm hello, the same question: "And how old are you Mrs. Schwartz?" "One hundred!" To which the rabbi responded, "Mrs. Schwartz, may the next twenty years be filled with health and happiness." Finally, he knocks on Mrs. Goldstein's door. "And how old are you, Mrs. Goldstein?" "Rabbi, today is my birthday! Today I am 120 years old." To which the rabbi replies, "Mrs. Goldstein, have a really great day!" When it comes to death, it is not a matter of "if," only a matter of "when," a when whose timing is hidden from us all. It is these two indisputable truths – death's inevitability and unpredictability – that are the working assumptions, the first principles, underlying the human condition.

But there also exists a third truth about our relationship to death, observed across time and traditions, and that is our disinclination to engage with the aforementioned first two truths. We are loath to do so, as if it is somehow untoward, morbid or even worse, will hasten the great foregone conclusion of our lives. You may recall the book published, coincidentally, exactly forty years ago this fall: *The Denial of Death* by Ernest Becker. Becker was a Jewish American cultural anthropologist, who, as an infantryman in WWII, was present at the liberation of the concentration camps – as close to the face of death as one could be. His Pulitzer Prize-winning book studied the consequences of what Freud described as the human tendency to repress death and the very thought of dying. "The idea of death," Becker wrote, "haunts the human animal like nothing else. It is a mainspring of human activity – activity designed largely to avoid the fatality of death, to overcome it by denying in some way that it is the final destiny for man." (p. ix). As individuals and as a society, we disguise death – problematically, even pathologically so – with all sorts of euphemisms and avoidance measures, as if to do so will enable us to escape the one most natural, shared and inevitable aspect of what it is to be human: death.

All of which is why today is so very important. Yom Kippur asks of us – or more precisely, demands of us – that we frequent that which we would rather avoid. My colleague and friend Marga Hirsch pointed out to me the fundamental difference between Yom Kippur and every other Jewish holiday, and it has nothing to do with the lack of whitefish. Every other holiday – Passover, Purim, Shavuot – you name it, calls on us to retrieve a past experience – the Exodus, the triumph over Haman, the giving of the Torah – to engage in it retrospectively, and apply its lessons to today. Yom Kippur alone calls on us to imagine the one prospective event we are all assured of, reflect on it, and then move forward that much wiser from the reconnaissance into our own mortality. It is a theological head fake, if you will, or better yet, a vaccination – enough to inoculate our character, but not the actual thing itself.

Someday I will teach a class on my favorite non-rabbinic philosopher, the sixteenth-century essayist, Michel de Montaigne; God knows, I quote him enough. In the early part of his life, Montaigne was obsessed by the oppressive weight of death. When he was thirty, his best friend died. Five years later, his father died. The following year his brother died in a freak sporting accident, and over time, he and his wife would lose four of their six children. The loss of his loved ones, the frequent and random manner by which they died – Montaigne was hounded by human mortality. But then something really unexpected happened. Montaigne himself almost died, thrown from his horse "like a thunderbolt," and he very nearly drifted into oblivion. (Sarah Bakewell, *How to Live*, p. 12-22) But Montaigne did not die – he lived. And not only did he live, but he came to understand his brush with death as an opportunity for a change in outlook, a new lease on life. In his own words:

> To begin depriving death of its greatest advantage over us, let us adopt a way clean contrary to that common one; let us deprive death of its strangeness; let us frequent it, let us get used to it . . . We do not know where death awaits us; so let us wait for it everywhere. To practise death is to practise freedom. A man who has learned how to die has unlearned to be a slave. (*Essays*)

In the years and writing to follow, Montaigne's near-death experience served as a pivot point to his identity. He realized that in avoiding his mortality, his anxiety had increased, but by confronting it, by "depriving death of its strangeness," as we do today, we actually affirm what life can be about. As Mark Twain would write years later: "The fear of death follows from the fear of life. A man who lives fully is prepared to die at any time." (Cited in Erica Brown, *Happier Endings*, p. 161)

This year, something totally unprecedented happened in my rabbinate, and as I have compared notes with my colleagues, theirs as well. Not infrequently, I am called by a congregational family and asked to recite *viddui* for a loved one – the confessional prayer we recite both today and on our deathbed, or as is often the case, recited by me on someone's behalf. The prayer asks that we forgive our loved ones, that they forgive us, so we can move forward into the next chapter with our conscience clean and our accounts balanced. Well, about nine months ago I received a call from the family of one congregant, let's call him Herb. It was no longer a matter of "if" but "when" and it was time for the rabbi to come down to the hospital for *viddui*. Sure enough there was Herb, in a scene I have seen more times than I can count: the IV, the morphine drip, the tracheal tube, the ventilator doing the breathing. Everyone understood – the family, the doctors – this was Herb's time. We gathered the family close, I recited *viddui*, we sang the *sh'ma* together and comforted each other into the night. Eventually, I gave the family the number of the funeral director, fully expecting Herb to pass before dawn. Everything was exactly as it should be, with one big exception: It is nine months later and Herb, God bless him, is still swinging. He didn't die that night. In fact, when I visited him last week, you should have seen his smile as I blew the shofar in his home! He is not out of the woods, not even close, but for the first time in my career, heaven would wait. May my deathbed prayer be equally ineffective for each and every one of you! I can't stop thinking about it, the theological curveball of having *viddui* said – and then living! For me, but more importantly, for Herb, it is an altogether delightful turn of events. Wiping the slate clean, having the chance to begin anew, and then, outwitting death. All of which is the theological calculus of today. As the tradition teaches: *Mitah v'yom ha-kippurim mit'khaprin*, Death and Yom Kippur bring atonement." To confess and cleanse, atone and forgive, press reset, and take a step forward knowing what we knew before but refused to acknowledge, that we are all on borrowed time and so we need to make the most of it.

For Montaigne, for Herb, for all of us, there can be a lightening of the soul that comes with the knowledge of the precious and precarious nature of our lives. To realize that death is as inevitable as it is unpredictable means that you are wise enough to know that life is not meant to be spent holding onto grudges, hatreds, and regrets. Rabbi Alan Lew tells the story of the famed Rabbi Shlomo Carlebach, who arrived in the States as a refugee from Austria, gained fame as a performer, touring widely, and later in life went back to give concerts in Austria and Germany. People would ask him, "How can you go back there and give concerts? Don't you hate them after what they did to you?" To which Rabbi Carlebach replied, "I only have one soul. If I had two souls, I would gladly devote one of them to hating the Germans full time. But I don't. I only have one soul, and I am not going to waste it on hating." (*This Is Real and You Are Completely Unprepared*, p. 230) Whether we come to shul today seeking to repent or to forgive, today reminds us that tomorrow may be too late. As the sage Rabbi Eliezer taught his students, we should repent one day before we die. His students, understandably, asked: "But does a person know on what day he will die?" Rabbi Eliezer replied: "All the more reason [to repent today] – lest one die tomorrow." (Babylonian Talmud, Shabbat 153a) Today is the day to let it go and more importantly, be courageous enough, big enough, to let other people do the same.

Yom Kippur's engagement with death is a clarifying agent, not just in terms of forgiveness, but also as a prompt for us all to recalibrate our priorities. As the Chofetz Chaim, Rabbi Israel Meir Kagan, once taught, life is like a postcard. We start writing casually in big letters until we find ourselves running out of room, scribbling smaller and smaller around the edges, trying to squeeze it all in. How many of us sit here in shul with that feeling in the pit of our stomach of knowing we are not living the lives of meaning we could be? Today we are asked to put the proverbial blank sheet of paper in front of us and map out what that life looks like: Our family, our careers, our communal and cultural commitments, our Judaism. Nobody has a magic wand, it takes time, it takes a lot of work, and – more often than not – a lot of pain to untangle ourselves from the knots we are presently in. But today is our chance to dream. In a sentence, that is what you are supposed to be doing in shul today! On Yom Kippur we are all akin to Reb Zusya. The Talmud records that on his deathbed Zusya explained to his disciples that what he feared most when he imagined arriving at the heavenly tribunal, was not that he would be asked why he did not live like Moses or Abraham or King David. What he feared most was what that he would be asked why he did not live like Zusya. Today we are more aware than ever of the dissonance between the life we lead and the life we should be leading, but unlike Zusya on his deathbed, we have been given a great gift – the gift of tomorrow.

Yom Kippur's brush with death is important because it prompts us to mend relationships; it is important because it jolts us into living the lives we should be living. But the most significant part of today's reconnaissance into death is that what we experience today only as a drill will one day be for real. When that day comes, all that will remain of us is the manner in which we are remembered and the legacy we leave for the future. As you can imagine, Lt. Colonel Shalev's heroism in the Yom Kippur War resulted in his being the recipient of every commendation you would expect. But what I didn't tell you is that he would receive those awards only posthumously. Why? Because two hours after he saved those thirty-three soldiers, in a battle totally unrelated to the one I described, Lt. Colonel Shalev was struck down and killed by enemy fire. Yom Kippur is here to remind us that while longevity has its place, none of us actually reach the Promised Land. We must, nevertheless, aspire to live lives worthy of others emulation. We can plant seeds whose harvest will be reaped well after our term on this earth. This is exactly the thought I had in mind a few months ago as I held Shalev's grandson – my friend's son – as he was named at his *bris* in memory of his heroic grandfather, Shaul Shalev of blessed memory. The spark of our humanity, limited in duration as it may be, is divine in that it contains the power to kindle other lives. As Hannah Senesh wrote in 1944 prior to her execution, after having parachuted behind enemy lines on behalf of her people:

> *Blessed is the match that was consumed but kindled flames.*
> *Blessed is the flame that burned in the secret places of the heart.*
> *Blessed are the hearts that knew how to cease beating honorably.*
> *Blessed is the match that was consumed but kindled flames.*

There is, no question, a singe to the message of Yom Kippur. But it is a singe that reminds us of the obligation, the opportunity, and the blessing in knowing that while the matches of our lives never burn as long as we would like, and they only ever burn once, it is within our power to live honorably, wisely, purposefully, and yes, joyfully, not only for ourselves, but also for the generations to follow.

The most beautiful sermon ever delivered at Park Avenue Synagogue was given by one of my predecessors, Rabbi Milton Steinberg, of blessed memory. It is called "To Hold with Open Arms," and he describes the experience of having suffered a massive heart attack and long hospitalization and then leaving the hospital. "I was permitted," he writes, "for the first time to step out of doors. And, as I crossed the threshold, sunlight greeted me. This is my experience – all there is to it. And yet, so long as I live, I shall never forget that moment." In that instant, basking in that glorious day, Steinberg remembered how too often in the past he had been indifferent to sunlight, to the laughter of his children, to the love of his wife. Too often he was preoccupied with petty concerns. He returned home wanting to say to husbands, to wives, to his congregants, to all those he met, and – I imagine, knowing as I do that when rabbis preach, they are really only preaching to themselves – to himself: "How precious is your lot in that it is one of love. Do not be, even for a moment, casual with your good fortune. Love one another while yet you may." Love your children, love your country, love your Jewish heritage. Hold and care for these precious things as closely as possible, but not too closely, for one day they will be surrendered to the Almighty. Embrace them, but do so with relaxed hands. Hold them, but with open arms.

Who will live and who will die? "None of us," wrote Alan Lew, "knows what will happen this year. Most of us will live, but some of us will die, and it might be me and it might be you. But whether we live or we die, we will only have one soul to do it with." (p. 235) Today may we forgive, may we love, may we nurture, and may we care for those singular and irreplaceable souls – our own, our loved ones', and those not yet born – holding them close in thought and deed, holding them with open arms.

Sh'mini Atzeret/Yizkor

Parting's Sweet Sorrow

More so than any other Jewish holiday, the meaning of today's festival of Sh'mini Atzeret is as enigmatic as it is elusive. "For seven days," commands Leviticus, you shall bring an offering unto God. But on the eighth day, it shall be a holy convocation for you, a day of *atzeret*," a day of cessation. (23:26). Adjacent to, but not part of Sukkot, Sh'mini Atzeret is connected neither to an historical event, nor to a specific agricultural occasion.

While theories abound, the loveliest explanation is offered by the eleventh-century commentator Rashi, who suggests that today's festival is best understood by way of a parable: A king invited his sons to feast with him for a number of days. Eventually, the time came for them to take leave of their father. The father – the king – implored his children, "Please, stay with me just one more day. It is difficult for me to part with you."

The message, the sentiment, is clear. Though tonight and tomorrow's finale of Simhat Torah remains, today we know that the festival cycle is winding down and we ourselves are preparing to leave. The haftarah we just chanted describes the return of worshippers at the Temple back to their homes. The prayer for rain, *Geshem*, which we will soon chant, is said no earlier than today, lest the journey of the returning pilgrims be ruined by wet weather as a result of our prayer. This pair of days signals our final pause before the sprint to Hanukkah, or as is the case in America, Thanksgiving. It has been a good holiday. And there is God, leaning over our shoulders as we check in to our flights back home, filled with the bittersweet sentiment of not wanting to let us go. "Stay for a while, my children Israel, I am not ready, let us linger a bit in our sweet sorrow."

In isolation, Rashi's parable, lovely as it may be, is also a bit provocative. The idea of God experiencing preemptive yearning at the prospect of being separated from loved ones is unexpected to say the least. God can be angry, even jealous, and hopefully forgiving, but are we really meant to believe that God experiences angst over letting go? And yet, if we flip back through the cycle of readings over this holiday season, again and again and again, it is exactly this sentiment to which we return. The first day of Rosh Hashanah, as Hagar faces the prospect of losing her son to the wilderness. The second day of Rosh Hashanah, as Abraham binds his beloved son Isaac on the altar, ready to let go of the very one he wanted most. And in the *haftarot*, Hannah, giving her child over to Temple service; and then Rachel, crying over her children as they went into exile. *Ha-ven yakir li Efraim, im yeled sha'ashu'im; ki midei dabri bo, zakhor ezk'renu od, al ken hamu mei'ai lo.* "Is Ephraim a darling son unto Me? Is he a child that is dandled? For as often as I speak of him, I do earnestly remember him still; therefore my heart yearns for him, I will surely have compassion upon him, says the Lord." (Jeremiah 31:20) Each one of these narratives, like the parable, hits the same emotional registry – the desire to hold on combined with the knowledge that we must let go, an exquisite and wrenching push and pull embedded at the core of the human experience.

This past August, while our own children were off at summer camp, Debbie and I hosted our annual send-off for the families of college-bound students. All the parents exchanged stories of the ease with which our children went off to camp or college and the emotional ordeal of being the parent left behind. Each separation, one parent related to me, was incremental preparation for the next more painful separation. But those separations, that parent went on to explain, are required if it is the growth of our beloved children that we are seeking. From the cutting of the umbilical cord right up to marriage itself, separation and self-reliance, letting go and growing up are necessary and interdependent steps in creating resilient, independent, and self-confident individuals. Not unlike – in fact, exactly like – in the Bible, from the limits of Eden to the border of the Promised Land, God's children venture forth into the unknown. Do we want to let go? Does God? Of course not. And the truth is, we never get used to it. But let go we must. So we resist and beg our loved ones to stay just for a short while more.

And now, as we arrive at Yizkor, we are asked to draw on a similar feeling. For what is true for our visits with the living is also true for the memories of the loved ones we recall today. The tablecloths, traditions, melodies, and memories of these holidays are being packed up. What is Yizkor if not the opportunity to linger for a time with the memories of our dearly beloved? Mothers and fathers, brothers and sisters, sons and daughters, husbands and wives – they are always in our thoughts. Their *yahrzeits* are annual reminders of the gaping loss left by their death. But today at Yizkor, especially on this day of Sh'mini Atzeret, we are asked to breathe in the memory of their lives, to dwell, as it were, in the sweet shadow of their abiding presence, and to reflect and appreciate how we continue to be shaped by the example they left. A quiet word of advice that continues to guide us. A commitment to a cause that we have now made one of our own priorities. An innocence of spirit or courage of heart that they were able to maintain, to which we will ever continue to aspire. Are there tears at Yizkor? Of course there are. But Yizkor is also a precious gift. It does not last forever. We savor this time to drink from the cup of memory, knowing that only too soon, we will, like the children in Rashi's parable, be on our way once again.

A final thought. Sh'mini Atzeret teaches us that as strong as our yearning for God may be, equally strong if not stronger is God's yearning for us. By extension, this moment of Yizkor similarly calls on us to draw close to the memory of our loved ones – jealous of every second – even in the awareness that it is fleeting. But maybe, perhaps, there exists a third quiet message of our Sh'mini Atzeret parable. God is still God and we are still God's children, but the feast refers not only to the festive season now passed, but to the passing season of our own mortality. What is life if not an invitation from the divine to enjoy the fruits of this world while we may? Psalm 27, the psalm of the season, expresses that each one of us seeks God's nearness, wanting nothing more than to be taken into God's dwelling. Our stay there, we know, will not be forever. As in the case of those we remember now, every life has its limits. God knows this better than anyone, and is likewise jealous for every moment we can be brought close to our Creator's presence. So we hear God's voice imploring us to draw near, to live as long as we can, as honorably as we can, as closely as we can, to the divine image in which we were created. Some day, one day, we will have to leave, and

God will have to let go. But until that time, we can grab hold of the memories of our loved ones and to the opportunity of our existence, and in doing so be assured that in the generations to come, it will be memories of each one of us that will be worthy to reside in the hearts and souls of those who will follow.

Ayekha?

Had Adam and Eve the presence of mind to invoke their Miranda rights in the Garden of Eden, the history of biblical religion, if not all of Western Civilization, might have turned out very differently.

Scarcely had they wiped the fruit off their lips, having just positioned their fig leaves in strategic locations, than they heard the sound of God breezing through the Garden. *Ayekha?* "Where are you?" God asks – the beginning of a deceptively simple, but altogether effective interrogation process. With a single question, the shortcomings not just of Adam but all of subsequent humanity were exposed, and ever since, our understanding of human nature has not been the same.

But the Miranda rights were not read and our story is not drawn from the annals of American criminal justice. God was not on a fact-finding mission. An omniscient God did not require Adam's confession in order to reconstruct what had just taken place. The Garden was not that big, and to the best of our knowledge, there were only two human beings for God to keep track of. God's question "Where are you?" was not about Adam's geographic coordinates, but about his moral location.

Welcome to the book of Genesis! A book about the creation of the world, the first families of the earth, the beginnings of humanity and the Jewish people, and ultimately how Israel ends up in the land of Egypt so they can be redeemed in the second book of the series, Exodus. Genesis is all that and much more, but the millennial traction of this book of beginnings is not merely its historical narrative, but its serving as a window into each and every one of our lives. Sibling rivalry and reconciliation, the challenge and miracle of conception, parental favoritism, leaving home and growing up, loss and grief, love found, delayed, and lost – you name it, most of human experience, good and bad, can be found right here. To read Genesis is not just to read of our founding matriarchs and patriarchs, or to study how the ancients understood the human condition. To read Genesis is to experience the unnerving sensation of feeling our own lives – mine and yours – refracted through the lens of our most sacred text.

There is no place better to begin than in the Garden itself. The first human being: part of, but distinct from, the rest of creation. God commands Adam to till and tend the Garden, encourages him to enjoy the fruit of every tree, except the tree of knowledge; from that tree he must not eat. The one becomes two with the creation of Eve, and then with the introduction of the serpent, two become three. To be sure, a talking serpent is not the easiest role to cast, especially for the rationalists in our midst. But what is clear is that at this point of the tale, competing impulses begin to emerge from within humanity. Not only does the appeal and imagined dividend of the single forbidden act grow, but the feared consequences of that act are brought into question. The transgressive behavior itself – eating the fruit – is simple and straightforward; sins usually are. But the Torah seems to take pleasure in elongating the process by which Eve arrives at the deed. "When the woman saw that the tree was good for eating and a delight to the eyes, and that the tree was desirable as source of wisdom, she took of its fruit and ate. She also gave some to her husband and he ate." (Genesis 3:6) It is almost as if – or more precisely, exactly as if – Eve does the very thing that we all do when given the opportunity to do something we know we should not do. Our moral defenses atrophy in the face of what we desire. We conveniently provide ourselves with newfound rationalizations and extenuating circumstances, all with the goal of tipping the scales of conscience towards making kosher that which we know is not. Even if it is wrong, it is not so wrong, certainly not just this once, not relative to the rationalizations in our minds.

And sometimes, oftentimes – as is the case in the Garden – when people do something wrong, despite what we are told as children or sometimes read in the papers, people do not get caught and people do not suffer immediate consequences. The serpent may be a lot of things, but let's not forget one thing: He was right. Not only was there a significant upside to eating the fruit, but the punishment foretold by God never took place. That is not to say there were no consequences. The text makes clear that immediately upon eating the fruit, Adam and Eve realized they were naked, *arum*, not insignificantly, the same Hebrew word that was used to describe the serpent a few verses earlier. Was this a punishment? At this point, apparently not. But their moral condition, at least in their own eyes, was – literally – laid bare. After all, with only two people in the whole world and an all-knowing God, who were they really hiding from, other than themselves? Adam and Eve knew they could not escape the one feeling that came not from above, but from within – the feeling we all have when we do something wrong – the feeling of shame.

All of this helps explain what happens in the next scene, when God draws Adam and Eve out of their moral bunker. God's questions here – and for that matter, with Cain in the next story – are phrased to elicit a response, and in both cases, humanity falls miserably short of divine expectations. Adam parries, ducks and dodges, passing the blame with both language and tactics that have remained fairly consistent to the present day. "That woman you gave me, she gave me of the tree and I ate." And the fairer sex does not fare much better. God asks Eve: "What is this you have done?" To which Eve replies, "It was the snake who tricked me, so I ate." Worst of all, we know, will be Cain, who attempts to redirect God's inquiry with the rhetorical question that has weighed on our collective conscience ever since, "Am I my brother's keeper?"

The more I think about it, the more I think that the sin of Adam and Eve was not eating from the tree. To repeat a terrible pun from my Bible professor Shalom Paul, this story is not about the "fruit on the tree" but about the "pair on the ground." Anyone could have predicted that left in the Garden as they were, their eating of the fruit was to be expected. The fifteenth-century Spanish Jewish philosopher Joseph Albo explained that their sin, the real sin of the Garden, was Adam and Eve's avoiding taking responsibility for their actions, Adam blaming Eve and then Eve blaming the serpent. (Cited in Sherwin, *The Life Worth Living*, p. 10) The offenses of our earliest ancestors, whatever they may have been, were compounded by their inability to stand accountable to themselves or to God, which is why the punishment for their misdeeds comes not after the act itself, but only after they fail to acknowledge any responsibility for what they did. Given the blessing of free will, the calculus of human nature is that on occasion, everyone will make a poor choice. That fact, in and of itself, does not distinguish a good person from a bad one. Rather, as the great philosopher Maimonides makes clear, it is a person's ability to admit failing, express remorse, and reform oneself for the future that signals moral growth and maturity.

As for the end of our parashah, on the most basic level, serpents lose their legs to become snakes, women experience pain in childbirth, and men must toil by the sweat of their brow. Remember, these stories are meant to explain the origins of the human condition. But on a more profound level, the lasting consequence of both Adam and Eve's act and that of Cain is to wander eastward forever separated from the Garden. Some take responsibility, some do not. Some are punished, many are not. But once we have eaten of the fruit and our eyes have been opened, none of us can reclaim the pristine naïveté of our former selves. Left to wander out in the world, we must be vigilant in protecting our moral selves from the impulses scattered throughout the world, but most of all within ourselves. When we fail, which we all inevitably will, we learn that honor comes not from the attainment of perfection, but from the ability to admit fault, to leverage regret towards self-improvement and from knowing that wherever on this earth we wander, God's first question continues to reverberate in our conscience: "Where are you?" *Ayekha?* In the year and years ahead, may each and every one of us heed the voice of the Garden – aware of our potential, admitting our shortcomings, and ever conscious of what it is to stand in the presence of God.

Noaḥ
Enlarging Your Heart

The most remarkable, most provocative and most self-evident premise of Biblical theology is the assertion that God cares at all about human beings. *Mah enosh*, "What is man, that you should take note of him?" The pointed question of the Psalmist goes to the heart of the matter: The humbling realization that relative to the grand scheme of the universe, each one of us, and all of us collectively, are miniscule – hardly deserving of divine attention. What an extravagant and counterintuitive claim it is to think that the same creator who set the moon and stars into motion, present at creation and throughout eternity, is at all mindful of our brief and insignificant existence!

Yet, we know, here in this sanctuary, that our entire system of belief rests upon this first principle. As we learned in last week's story of creation, not only were we the final and crowning achievement of the six days of creation, but we were created in the very image of God, each one of us, in all our individuality, a reflection of our Creator, infused with the divine spark. Our actions – our mitzvot – are thus expressive of our relationship with God. Our prayers, we believe, are worthy of God's attention, and the world in which we live operates in the sphere of divine concern. God may not walk in the Garden with us as with Adam and Eve, but if the Torah teaches us anything, it teaches that our God is involved and invested in our lives. God cares – deeply – about each and every one of us.

And when we mess up – oh boy, does God get upset! That, I believe, is the most unexpected part of this week's Torah reading. It is not the least bit surprising that mankind is corrupt and lawless. It is also statistically plausible that despite the base condition of humanity at large, an ethical outlier named Noaḥ, a man of great righteousness, could emerge. But what is surprising, what is downright startling, is that God gets really, really upset about it. "And the Lord saw how great man's wickedness on earth, and how every plan of man's heart is evil . . . And the Lord regretted that He had made man on earth and his heart was saddened. The Lord said, "I will blot out from the earth the humanity I created." (Genesis 6:5-8) OK, so we were bad, maybe even really bad, maybe even a whole bunch of us. But really? Are we really to think that an omnipotent, omniscient, and presumably rather busy God lets the little things get him down? Are the failings of humanity really worthy of God's fury?

It is a good question, but it is a question whose answer lies not in the stars, but in ourselves. Remember, each one of us is created in God's image. Can any of us dare claim not to have done exactly the same? How very easy it is to allow a hurt, a slight, a disappointment – even those, especially those, that are so trivial as to not even merit our concern – to grow to absorb the entirety of our being. A call isn't returned, an unkind word hits us roughly, a situation is fumbled, an appointment is missed. I am not talking about big hurts; in fact my very point is the inverted relationship between the minor nature of the hurt and the overblown size of our concern. The garden variety, petty, inevitable and daily kind, that instead of shrugging off as the unavoidable consequence of being a card-carrying member of a flawed humanity, instead of admitting that we ourselves have been late, insensitive, or forgetful too, instead of choosing to transcend or move beyond the circumstances of a less than perfect exchange, we do just the opposite. Not only do we linger unnecessarily in the hurt, but we stew in it and insist on finding a hidden motive or ill intent. Minimally, we convince ourselves that whatever the hurt, from that moment forth, it eclipses the entirety of a relationship. We do not do what we know we would ask others to do if the tables were turned; we do not "get over it."

How is it that God becomes so exasperated with a flawed humanity? It would seem, at least in these early Biblical stories, God lacked the one ingredient that makes life livable: perspective. Don't get me wrong, anger has its place, but I think misplaced anger can usually be traced back to those moments when we lack or lose perspective on the bigger picture, where our circle of concern really lies, and our entire field of vision becomes blocked by some infraction beneath the dignity of our attention. Our hearts constrict, our mood tightens, and not surprisingly, we respond with the one and only arrow left in our depleted emotional quiver: anger. Were there other remedies at the God's disposal? Presumably so. Did the punishment fit the crime? Probably not. But none of that mattered. In the absence of perspective, reason melted away, to be replaced by an all-consuming anger, and thus, as we know, the terrible flood began.

All of which, I think, helps us understand how the story ends. The fascinating thing about this Torah reading, what we often miss, is that there is absolutely no change in the human condition, no moral development, between the time before the flood and the time after it. In fact, when the waters have subsided, God makes pretty much the same observation about the hard wiring of human beings as before the flood: "Every plan of man's heart is evil." And because there is no lesson learned for Noah or humanity as a whole, we know this story is really about the other main character – God. It is in God's personality that character development takes place. God knows that humanity will sin again, but as the sky clears, God sets the rainbow in the heavens, declaring, "When the rainbow is in the clouds, I will see it and remember the everlasting covenant between God and all creatures." (Genesis 9:16) In other words, the rainbow was and would remain the self-help tool by which God could gain the perspective that God was lacking at the beginning of the story. Knowing humanity's endless capacity for wickedness, and knowing that disengaging was not an option, God needed to establish a reminder as long as a rainbow, in order that God's anger would never again overwhelm, that God's love and kindness would always win out. In other words, God enlarged the divine heart. Never again would humanity's shortcomings consume the entirety of the divine being.

It has been exactly this way ever since. One of my favorite *midrashim*, rabbinic legends, tells of God's time management skills. For a third of the day, not surprisingly, God takes out the Torah and studies. Another third of the day, God serves as the cosmic matchmaker, bringing couples together. And in the final third, God serves as cosmic judge and administrator. The text goes on to explain that upon entering the courtroom, knowing the challenge ahead, God recites the following prayer: "May it be My will that My love for humanity overcomes My exasperation with them!" It seems that the struggle never ends. Every single day God prays for a heart capable of stretching, filled with a *ḥesed*, a kindness, that will offset the daily frustrations humanity provides.

This is, I believe, what each and every one of us must aspire towards ourselves. The Talmud teaches that a person is known by three things: *b'koso, b'kiso, b'ka'aso*, by the way one drinks, by the way one spends money, and by the way one manages anger. (Eruvin 65) The first two are worthy of a sermon for another day and make sense intuitively. The third measure – how one does or doesn't get angry – is, I believe, the most sensitive window into what makes a person tick. As is taught in *Pirkei Avot*, the Ethics of our Fathers, the highest rung of character is reserved for the person who is slow to anger and easy to pacify – that is the *ḥasid*. No matter what other qualities we may possess, it is our ability to have emotional and relational perspective that determines how far we will go in our lives. We need look no further than the greatest of all our leaders, Moses; were it not for his anger – in striking the rock – he would have entered the Promised Land. Ultimately, the sages explain, an angry person has nothing other than his anger (Babylonian Talmud, Kiddushin 40b); or to put it slightly more colloquially, each one of us must learn how to expand our hearts, fill them with kindness, and not let the things we can't control, control us.

With every passing day, I find myself drawn more and more to Abraham Joshua Heschel's remark: "When I was young I admired clever people. Now that I am old, I admire kind people." Some people are born with brains, others with looks, others with beautiful voices and others with great outside jump shots. Some people, over the course of their lives work hard to arrive at circumstances that determine a successful path in life. But being kind – that is also hard. Being kind takes a lot of work, it takes a lot of patience, it takes a lot of deep breathing and most of all, it means an endless reservoir of perspective. To be kind is a commitment that has to be renewed every single day, if not every single minute, with every single person we meet. It is a mental discipline whereby we learn not only to remove anger from our hearts, but to possess hearts large enough to endure the wear and tear of what it is to be human. It is something that even God has to work on daily. It is a quality, as Heschel understood, that we should not only admire, but as creatures created in God's image, should aspire towards ourselves.

Va-yera

Radical Hospitality

H ad the Pew Research Center analyzed the condition of the
Jewish community of this week's parashah, their assessment
would undoubtedly have been altogether gloomy, if not
downright bleak. Relative to the general population, the Jewish community as represented by Abraham and Sarah suffered a desperately
low fertility rate. It was an aging demographic of two, Abraham at
ninety-nine and Sarah not far behind. Even back then, one of every
two unions, Sarah and then Hagar, was with a non-Jew. In terms of the
structural impediments to living an active Jewish life, considering last
week's story of circumcision, I would characterize the bar of entry as
pretty high. As for the percentage of Jews who would identify themselves as religious, given Isaac's near sacrifice on the altar, we can excuse his generation's understandable lapse in God-talk. How strong
was this generation's attachment to the Promised Land? Last I checked,
as much of this story takes place outside of Israel as in it. Had a survey
been conducted back then, I imagine the Jewish press would have char-
acterized the results as dour if not dire. Had a survey been conducted
back then, I imagine anyone reading the coverage would have been
sure that the first study of Jewry would also be the last.

Of all the questions I have pondered since the results of the recent
Pew Survey on American Jewry were released, high on my list has been
the question of why I have avoided speaking about it. Sermon after sermon from my colleagues, one conference call after another, panel after
panel, and more op-eds in the Jewish press, it would seem, than self-
identifying Jews – the survey has raised more questions than it has
sought to answer. How was the data collected? How were the questions framed? Is it accurate? Do one percent of Orthodox Jews really

have Christmas trees? And even if we accept the information, what does it mean for the Jews? Most people interpret the data with great pessimism, the study an alarming wake-up call for a community on the decline. Others see the silver lining in all the data, insistent that there is good news to be found. Part of my hesitation, I think, is my knowing that our narrative on the Upper East Side is very different from what is taking place nationally. Consider today: a double day-school bar mitzvah, a filled sanctuary, filled hallways, and filled classrooms of intellectually, spiritually, and philanthropically engaged Jews. Take a trip outside of this neighborhood and you will understand the bubble we live in. Just this week, I heard of a colleague being laid off, as a historic Midwest synagogue prepares to shut its doors. I know exactly what is going on outside of our bubble, and it strikes me as somehow unseemly to weigh in on the tough times of American Jewry from a pulpit and community enjoying such bounty.

The more fundamental reason I think I have avoided speaking about the survey is that I am a congregational rabbi and not a sociologist, and as a rabbi I am not exactly sure how all the analyzing actually helps push the conversation forward. As Mark Twain once remarked about the weather, everyone is talking about it, but nobody is doing anything about it. As a rabbi toiling in the trenches of Jewish life, my question is always about you, the Jew in the pew, and what makes you tick. Don't get me wrong, there is a time and place for fancy folk with fancy titles to sit on long-term planning committees to assess data and allocate Jewish communal resources. Sometimes I even get to sit in on those conversations. But here in this room, we know that not only is all religion local, but it is deeply personal. The decision to affiliate – or not. To come to shul – or not. To observe mitzvot – or not. To go to Israel – or not. These and a million other markers of active Jewish existence are decisions that this institution is trying to impact every day. With a limited amount of time in a rabbinical day, or for that matter, lifetime, I would rather spend it thinking about how to bring Jews closer to Torah, closer to God, and closer to each other. It is not at all clear to me that the massive amount of time and energy being spent debating the study will bring any Jews closer to their spiritual inheritance, and that is where I think we here in this room need to spend our time.

Which brings us back to Abraham. I believe that it is in the figure of Abraham, more than in any op-ed, where the secret of Jewish continuity lies. There he sat, at the beginning of this week's parashah, in the heat of the day, ready to greet a wayfarer from any direction. The rabbis comment that his placement is itself an indication of his character; that despite his vaunted spiritual stature, he sat humbly at the tent door greeting the passing stranger. And when one would come by – as did the three visitors – out he ran, *ratz likratam*, to greet them. Were these passersby mere men or emissaries from the divine? It is not exactly clear, but that is the point. As Franz Rosenzweig noted on this passage long ago, "Abraham is the religious man par excellence for he sees God in the human situation." Abraham's spiritual greatness was that he saw God's image in everyone, friend, stranger, or otherwise. It was not the externals that interested Abraham; in Abraham's mind everyone possessed a spark of the divine. Abraham embodied what Ron Wolfson calls a form of "radical hospitality," what is called in Hebrew *hakhnasat orḥim*. (*Relational Judaism*) In Abraham's presence everyone felt welcome, everyone felt embraced. And you know what? Despite the aforementioned tongue-in-cheek trends that would have argued otherwise, Abraham's open spiritual posture worked and he reaped huge rewards. He became *av-raham*, the father of many, making souls, *oseh n'fashot*, our outreach role model ever since.

Because I believe that the human soul has remained essentially constant since the Bible, I also believe that those concerned for the Jewish future need look no further than the Abrahamic model to respond to our present angst. You want to know who the most thrilling religious leader of our era is? The new Pope, Pope Francis. Why? Because some six months into his papacy, the Pontiff has performed the canonization-worthy PR miracle of overhauling the public's perception of the Vatican. No longer does the church lead with its chin, letting a list of "Thou shalt nots" define its mission. No longer is the church asking the question "Who is out?" but rather "Who is in?" From his headline-grabbing comment on homosexuality "Who am I to judge?" to his more recent comment that that Church had grown obsessed with abortion, gay marriage, and contraception, this Pope understands the big tent needs of the hour. Significantly, if you study his words closely, the shift is one of style not substance. There have been no doctrinal revolutions, no policy changes, no line dancing in St. Peter's Square. As Pope John XXIII stated at the opening of the Second Vatican Council, the deposit of faith is one thing; "the way in which it is presented is another." But think of how far the tone has changed since the "God's Rottweiler" days of Pope Benedict. It is far too early to count the returns, but as Timothy Egan recently wrote, Pope Francis' expansive and embracing vision has resulted in the emergence of a Catholic community that though "lapsed" is now very much "listening."

It is from this playbook that we, as a Jewish community, should learn a lot – very, very quickly. Whatever the assumptions of mid-century middle America may have been, I don't need a study to tell me that it is no longer the case. The most famous book on American religious sociology of the 1950s was Will Herberg's *Protestant-Catholic-Jew*, a book whose very title speaks to its assessment that American religious life was composed of three steady streams of inherited religious affiliation. If your parents were Irish or Italian, that meant you would be Catholic and would affiliate with the Church, as would Jews with Jews and synagogues, and Protestants with Protestants and churches. But the time for any automatic tribal affiliation has long since passed. This week I had lunch with a proud, self-identified Jew, who over the years has given more time and support to the Jewish world than most people in their lifetime. Over the meal he joyfully shared that his children were joining a synagogue. And because I can't help myself, I asked him, "So who called the synagogue and who is paying for the membership?" On both counts, he replied that it was he. It was the smallest exchange that spoke volumes about what is taking place nationally. The default assumption that one joins, affiliates, and supports Jewish institutional life – simply because that is what Jews do – is a language that has lost its traction. And that has nothing to do with Jewish or Catholic, nothing to do with Orthodox, Conservative, or Reform – that is the just the fact of religion in America today.

All of which is why, when formulating a response to concerns for Jewish continuity, we need to think not just locally, not just personally, but inter-personally. On more than one occasion, I have shared how it was one individual who stopped me as I was walking out of my campus Hillel who triggered my journey back into Jewish life and living. If you see Jewish communities that are growing, that are thriving on campus, in the city, in the suburbs, or anywhere, I am willing to bet that at the heart of these communities lies the radical hospitality, the open spiritual posture practiced by Abraham. As Martin Buber once noted, "All real living is meeting." It has nothing to do with ideology. It is not Orthodox or Conservative, it doesn't matter if you are a store-front start-up or Park Avenue Synagogue. It is the small and simple gesture of recognizing the humanity of the person sitting next to you, not judging them because they are taller or shorter, or older or younger, or richer or poorer, or more or less religious. They are human beings created in the image of the divine just as you are. In welcoming them warmly, you designate them, this sanctuary, and our faith as sacred. As the book of Proverbs teaches, "The soul of a person is the candle of God." (20:27) Each one of us, like a candle, can kindle the flame of another soul without diminishing the strength of our own flame. What is the secret to creating vibrant Jewish communities? Welcome everyone, invest in everyone, greet everyone, make everyone feel that their presence matters. There is no shortage of challenges facing the Jewish world, but if you want to know what you personally can do to help facilitate Jews to join, affiliate, and support Jewish institutions, practice radical hospitality. That is the secret to the Jewish future.

The late Rabbi Shlomo Carlebach was once asked to describe his ideal community, a community that would, in 1960s San Francisco, become known as the House of Love and Prayer. Famously, he responded by characterizing his ideal community as one where when you arrive, people are happy to see you, and when you leave, people miss you. At any given moment there are people walking in and walking out of this building and by extension, Jewish life. More likely – and increasingly, it would seem – they are walking right by it, opting not to stop in at all. We need to sit at the opening of the tent, literally and figuratively, even running out to greet them. We need to spend less time worrying about Pew research and more time connecting with the people we would like to have sitting in the pews. We need to do the very thing Abraham started doing so long ago. In doing so, no matter what the pundits say, we will fulfill the ancient promise made to him: that our people should grow as numerous as the stars in the sky and the sands of earth, a blessing for all to behold.

Parenting

Considering that I am just under one month shy of my oldest daughter's bat mitzvah, it may strike you (as it does me) as a bit presumptuous for me to deliver a sermon about parenting. The returns, as they say, are not yet in. Proud as I am of each of my children, caution, common sense, and a bit of humility would counsel me to wait a few more years before weighing in on matters on which, I readily concede, so many in this room have spent many more years – and tears – than I have.

But then again, were it the case that a rabbi must have definitive knowledge of a subject in order to preach on that subject, the archives of Jewish preaching would be a lot smaller. The problem of evil, the meaning of life, whether God hears our prayers, the Middle East – the most impenetrable and imponderable issues – these are the subjects about which we are asked to speak week in and week out. And what imponderable is more imponderable than child rearing? Nevertheless, if the qualification to weigh in on a subject is to have engaged with the question with sincerity and persistence, then by this count I have earned the right to share a word or two this morning.

When it comes to parenting, it is not as if our ancestors were any better at it than we are! Adam raised a Cain; Noah fared little better with his children. Abraham and Sarah: one child, Ishmael, cast into the wilderness, and the other, Isaac, bound on the altar. Would it have been too much to ask of God to provide parenting classes for the progenitors of an entire people?

Of all the biblical couples whose parenting model serves as an example of what *not* to do, none stand out more than the patriarch and matriarch of this week's parashah: Isaac and Rebecca. In fact, the father of modern Orthodoxy, Samson Raphael Hirsch, plainly stated that the take-home of this week's family saga of the fraternal strife between Jacob and Esau is actually a counterexample, a signpost for parents of what not to do in their own households! So many blunders: Isaac's favoring of Esau; Rebecca's showering her love on Jacob. Hirsch points to how Isaac and Rebecca broke the golden rule of parenting, *ḥanokh l'naar al pi darkho*, bring up each child in accordance with his or her own way. Not only did Isaac and Rebecca foist their own foibles and insecurities upon their children, but they stifled their children's individual natures by prematurely telegraphing the trajectory of their lives. And if this was not enough, the text provides no indication whatsoever that Isaac and Rebecca communicated or collaborated in raising their children. As parents they were "siloed off" from one another, with the children never receiving a coherent or consistent message. Is it at all surprising that with parents like them, the children grew up individually confused, fraternally at cross-purposes, and collectively – as a family unit – totally dysfunctional?

The particular parenting flaws of Isaac and Rebecca are as numerous as they are deep. But were I to single out the foundational problem, it would be that the two of them represent two very different parenting modalities, each one problematic, and all the more so when working at cross-purposes. On the all-important question of how much or how little a parent structures, intervenes, and participates in a child's development, Isaac and Rebecca are at opposite ends of the spectrum. Consider Isaac. From the very first scene when Rebecca pleads with him to address the agony of her pregnancy to the final scene, when Isaac is duped into giving the wrong blessing, there is something totally passive and removed about Isaac's relationship with his children. "Fetch me some game, prepare for me a dish," Isaac directs Esau. Yes, Isaac is old, but one senses that it is not only a diminished physicality limiting Isaac's movement, but a withdrawn nature, an emotionally sequestered aspect of his being that we know will have weighty consequences in the chapters to come.

And then there is Rebecca, who – with her white-knuckle grip on the affairs of her household – is at the opposite end of the spectrum. She choreographs the entire family drama with precision, manipulating her husband, inducing Jacob to betray his brother, and then, seeing Esau's rage, engineering Jacob's safe flight from home. Rebecca gives new meaning to William Wallace's notion that "the hand that rocks the cradle is the hand that rules the world." Scripting and executing without a hiccup, she directs every aspect of her children's life.

With enough time, we could probably pinpoint the moment in Isaac's youth that resulted in his nature as a parent. So too, I imagine that Rebecca, having been brought up in Laban's household, had good reason to take such a hands-on approach to her family. But regardless of the causes, it is evident that the consequences of their disparate approaches were devastating. Removed from the affairs of his children, Isaac abdicates control of his boys, and not surprisingly, things go off the rails, leaving him with one son fuming and one son who has left home altogether. And while Rebecca's plan proves effective in the short term and the long term, her shadow looms heavily over the rest of Jacob's life. We know that in the following chapter, Jacob will be duped by his father-in-law, and then, tragically, show himself to be totally ineffective in facing the subsequent trials of his own children: first the rape of Dinah and then the sale of Joseph to Egypt. For the rest of his life, Jacob lacked the tools to confront the challenges that awaited him. In the weeks ahead, it will be the events of this week's parashah that we will reference to understand Jacob's recurring flaw. Jacob never developed the coping tools he would need in the years ahead. Why should he and how could he? His mother always did everything for him.

From this initial paradigm of parenting in the Bible right up to today, not a whole lot has changed. The world is divided into tiger mothers and duct tape parents. There are those who believe that we must take a Rebecca-like, aggressive, interventionist approach to raising our children – serving as their advocates, cheerleaders, coddlers, and disciplinarians – helicoptering in to defend them at every turn. And there are those who counsel just the opposite – that we must let things play out, allow our children to skin their knees, or as one book counsels, duct tape our mouths shut, our feet to the ground, restrain ourselves, control our urge to intervene. (Wendy Mogel, *The Blessing of a Skinned Knee*; Vicki Hoefle, *Duct Tape Parenting*) To do otherwise – as with Jacob under Rebecca – denies our children the tools to solve problems on their own, which they will one day, inevitably, be called on to do.

Whether it is Isaac and Rebecca or the current literature on the

subject, neither extreme, we know, is acceptable. The Talmud in Tractate Kiddushin enumerates the mitzvot that every parent is obligated
to perform for children. For boys, a *bris* at eight days; for firstborns, a
pidyon haben at thirty days. We are obligated to teach our children
Torah or pay for their Jewish education. As the list goes on, it gets more
interesting, including the obligation to teach your child a trade, find
your child a mate, and teach your child to swim. Our world is different than the one of the Talmud, the issues and intervals of our day are
different, but the guiding ethic must be the same. Parenting calls on us
to perform those acts which generational, financial, or moral consid-
erations obligate us to provide, but also to recognize an equal obligation to create self-reliant, self-starting, self-sufficient, and autonomous
human beings. It is not either/or. There is a time for the tactic of Isaac,
just as there may be a time for that of Rebecca, but good parenting is
not one or the other. Good parenting is having the wisdom to differentiate one muscle group from the other, and having the courage to
"look long" in deciding which one we choose, understanding that our
present decisions will have ramifications well beyond this moment.

As I am sure is true for every parent in this room, there is nothing
in this world – nothing – that I care about more or love more deeply
than my children. As their parent, I make no apologies for insisting
that so long as they live in our house, they abide by our value system.
But I also know that at the end of the day, my goal as a parent is that
they will have the self-esteem and self-efficacy to navigate this world
once I have, so to speak, left the room. If we want our boys to be good
husbands, our girls to be good wives, our children to be good Jews, the
next generation to establish lives and families of meaning and purpose,
not only will they have to stumble a few times along the way, but each
one of us will have to loosen our grip to enable them to arrive at their
full potential. And when all else fails, we must remember that the most
important and enduring impact any of us have on our children is not
what we tell them to do, but what they see us do. It is the unfolding
model of our own lives that is actually the curriculum from which our
children learn the most.

In reference to this week's Torah reading, Rabbi Art Green cites the
eighteenth-century Hasidic sage, Rabbi Dov Ber, the Maggid of Mez-
erich, who explains that there are two kinds of love a parent has for a

child. The first love, biological or physiological in nature, is a byproduct of the bond between parent and child. This is the bullet we take for our children, the lengths we would go to ensure their safety, security, and well-being. But there is also a second love, a greater love, and that is the love a parent experiences upon seeing a child find his or her stride, go on the right path, live righteously and wisely. (*Speaking Torah*, p. 116) It is the exquisite feeling of seeing our children find their way, informed by our model even if their path veers from the one we have chosen in our own lives. It is not either/or. Our hearts must be sufficiently capacious, supple, and textured to house both loves. May we all be wise enough to appreciate both, draw on both, and please God, enjoy both into the years ahead.

Vayishlaḥ

Rachel's Tears

In my entrance exam for rabbinical school, I was asked to recite the Talmudic debate on the proper sequence of family and career. As formulated by the gendered language of the Talmud: "What should a man do first, get married or study Torah?" Not surprisingly, the Rabbis disagreed. Some Rabbis argued that a person should first study Torah, and only then get married. Rav Yehuda, on the other hand, stated in the name of Rav Shmuel that a person should first get married, and only then study Torah. I clearly recall reciting to my examiner Rabbi Yoḥanan's retort to Rav Shmuel's position: *Riḥayim b'tzvaro, v'ya'asok ba-torah?* "With a millstone around his neck, can he study Torah?" In other words, how can someone be expected to commit to their studies when laden down by the burdens of family life? Rabbi Yoḥanan thus agreed with the first opinion: One should first study and only then look to marry. As confusing as this debate may be, what is even more confusing are the rationales ascribed to the respective sides.

According to the medieval commentator Rashi, because the men of Babylonia would travel to Israel to study, they could focus on Torah free of family burdens (and, incidentally, lustful thoughts) and should therefore get married prior to leaving for study abroad. The men of Israel, however, who remained in Israel to study, should study first and only then get married. Were they to do otherwise, they would (as Rabbi Yoḥanan reasoned) be unable to focus on Torah with family in such close proximity. To make matters yet more confusing, the next generation of medieval commentators after Rashi, known as the Tosafot, offer exactly the opposite rationale. Namely, they say it is precisely those who travel from place to place who should not marry first, for were they to do so, they would long for their family left at home to the detriment of their studies. And it is precisely those who study near where they live who should go ahead and marry and then study. (Babylonian Talmud, Kiddushin 29b)

Despite having passed that oral exam, I still find the particulars of that Talmudic argument somewhat confusing. My confusion is not simply because the arguments and rationales across the rabbinic generations are difficult to track and untangle. My confusion stems from the fact that to this day, the issue remains very, very confusing. In more egalitarian language, what should a person do first: family or career? What is the right sequence for us, and more importantly, for our children? Is it better first to find a mate, start a family, produce one, two, three, or more kids? Or just the opposite? Get credentialed, get settled, get established, and then and only then lift your head up and start looking for your *beshert*? As muddled and divided as the rabbis of the Talmud may have been on this issue, can any of us in this room, in this age, claim to have come up with a definitive answer?

I would claim that the debate continues unabated. The texts may not have the sanctity of a page of Talmud, but we need only look to two recent newspaper articles to see the flashpoints of this same conversation playing out today. The first article – you may recall it – appeared last summer in the Princeton campus paper, the *Daily Princetonian*. It was a letter from the mother of a male student advising campus women to "Find a husband on campus before you graduate." "You will never again," she wrote, "have this concentration of men who are worthy of you." On and off campus, the letter stirred a firestorm of response, some praising the author for taking a courageous position on an "untouchable" subject and many, not surprisingly, assailing the author for her obnoxious, ill-considered, and retrograde counsel to Princeton women and, by extension, achievement-seeking women everywhere.

The second article, a little more recent, a little closer to home, was a *New York Times* article about the dating habits of women at the University of Pennsylvania. The article described a culture in which campus women are so driven to academic and professional achievement that they have opted out of the burdensome emotional entanglements of committed relationships, preferring a hook-up culture of casual sexual encounters. Aside from resulting in a spike in applications to Penn this fall, this article also provoked a huge stir. Were we to accept the claims of the article (which many do not), is it a good thing or a bad thing to see conventional notions of sexuality overturned so that women can be all that they can be? Both the Princeton and Penn articles brought into relief all the gender double standards that are applied to the challenge of balancing relationships and professional achievement. Implicit in the Penn article is the assumption that there is something titillating in the discovery that women's sexuality can function the same as men's. Would there have been anything remotely interesting, the thinking goes, about an article describing a campus culture where men engage in casual relationships as they unflinchingly aspire to professional success?

I could go on, but the ultimate point is not whether you think these articles are good or bad, accurate or not. The point is that these articles somehow hit a nerve in our collective psyche, touching third-rail questions that we don't like talking about, questions that we dodge and duck, but whose answers play out in all our families and thus in the broader Jewish community. We want our children to be accomplished. We want our children to gain higher degrees. We want our children to pursue their careers. We also want our children to find their *beshert*. We want our children to marry a Jew. We want our children to give us Jewish grandchildren. We want a whole lot of things, and for that matter, so do our children. Then one day we wake up and discover that – lo and behold – we can't always get what we want. To use the rabbinic aphorism: *tafasta meruba lo tafasta*, if you try to grab too much, you run the risk of not grabbing anything at all.

For the last month we have been bombarded with article after article about the Pew study, specifically the shrinking non-Orthodox American Jewish population. Of all the analysis and articles, I'll give you two statistics that will make you sit up. First, the fertility rate for non-Orthodox Jews is 1.7 as against a Zero Population Growth requirement of 2.1, meaning we are not reproducing at a stable or steady rate. Second, the intermarriage rate among non-Orthodox Jews has risen to 72 percent. Yes, you heard that number correctly: 72 percent. It does not take a rocket scientist, or even a mediocre sociologist, to figure out that if people put off marriage until later, put off child rearing until later, there are consequences to those choices. These statistics are not unique to the Jewish world. A rise in delayed marriage or non-marriage, a decline in fertility – these trends cross faith lines. It is precisely for this reason that those of us invested in the Jewish future need to appreciate the bigger picture of which we are but a representative part. Since the Pew study came out, the entire Jewish world has been thrown into a frenzy of soul searching and finger pointing over how best to address a contracting Jewish world. Some say we should circle the wagons, others that we should widen the tent. Some argue we should throw our efforts into the denominational movements, others that we should throw the movements out altogether. Let me boil it down to a sentence coined by my friend and colleague Professor Steven M. Cohen: *Im ein yehudim, ein yahadut.* "If there are no Jews, there is no Judaism." Intermarriage, low fertility – these are merely the symptoms of underlying systemic or structural conditions on which we continue to punt. And then we have the hutzpah to point fingers at everyone and everywhere, except of course for the demographic elephant standing in the middle of the room.

Let me pause for a second and be very clear about what I am saying and what I am not saying, and let me say it with great sensitivity. After all, this conversation lies at the existential core of so many of us. I am not saying that our young men and women must choose between professional or familial fulfillment. I also know enough to know that this choice is not altogether in their hands for them to make. I know, and so do you, that there are many in this world, many in this room, for whom the dream and desire to raise a family is for one reason or another painfully elusive. Would that wanting it were all it took to make it so! And similarly, there are many in this room who have understandably correlated professional achievement with personal fulfillment, and go to sleep at night or wake up in the morning asking themselves all sorts of painful questions of self-worth. Nobody knows – not you and certainly not me – the juggling acts and internal struggles embedded in the person sitting next to you. So let's agree that when we speak on this matter, we will do so with great sensitivity.

During my years at the University of Chicago, I had an academic setback that resulted in a delay in my receiving my PhD. It was a crazy time of life for me – juggling a rabbinate, pursuit of a doctorate, and one child after another being born. Something was bound to give and eventually it did. I remember sitting totally deflated in the office of my advisor, who shared her sage advice: "Elliot, I don't know if you will or won't get everything you want in life, but I am pretty sure you won't get it all at the same time." Life, she counseled, was not always to be lived simultaneously, but sometimes sequentially. I licked my wounds, regrouped, recalibrated the road map, and picked myself up in order to march forward. All our lives have such inflection points; some behind us and most likely many yet to come. Some choices we get to make and some choices are made for us. The circumstances of our existence are not always ours to determine and more often than not, a lot just comes down to *mazel*, to luck.

But just because we can't control everything, just because it is a sensitive issue, doesn't mean we shouldn't talk about it. We have to talk about it and more importantly we have to do something about it! Let's start a community conversation on the most prickly issue of the day. Let's speak openly about how to balance family and career. What is the corrective to our presently bipolar world that seeks to recreate an Ozzie-and-Harriet-like "golden age of marriage" in a time and place that is anything but? How is it that we live in a country that does not see universal day care as a moral imperative? How is it that the Jewish community tells families to produce more than 2.1 kids, send those children to Jewish day schools and Jewish summer camps, hold down two jobs, and also be home for dinner? What would a Jewish conversation look like that offered differentiated and equal visions of gender roles? How do we go about creating a synagogue culture that fully embraces single parents, gay parents, multi-racial and multi-ethnic parents – any parents or families that look a little different than Great Neck in the 1950s? How do we go about establishing a communal norm and funding structure whereby non-Orthodox kids could take not just ten days, but a full gap year in Israel with the implicit or explicit goal of creating more and more Jewish couples? Most of all, what does it mean to raise children capable of understanding that sometimes life is either/or and sometimes life is both/and, and sometimes the choices we make for ourselves are different than the choices others make for themselves, and that is OK, because all of us are just trying to do the best we can. We don't need to have it all figured out overnight; generations of rabbinic sages have struggled with the same questions. But we do need to stop doing what we have been doing – avoiding the conversation. We deserve better, our children deserve better, and our actual or idealized grandchildren – they definitely deserve better.

The most enduring image of this week's Torah reading is the heartbreaking death and burial of our matriarch Rachel. Her husband Jacob had toiled for years before they could finally marry. "Give me children, or I shall die," she cried during those first years of marriage, as she endured round after round of unfulfilled dreams. The name of her long-awaited son Joseph derived from the Hebrew meaning "God has taken away my shame." Now, tragically, she dies in childbirth, buried on the side of the road – on the outskirts of present-day Jerusalem – to this day a holy site for those praying for children. The book of Jeremiah describes her weeping as the children of Israel, exiled into Babylon, pass by her grave. It is a weeping that we pray will one day be replaced by laughter and joy as the depleted ranks of her children are replenished.

Rachel's tears bear witness to our ancient and ongoing fears for the next generation of Jews, and it would seem that these days those tears are justifiably flowing more freely. We could, and perhaps should, visit her tomb and offer prayers. But I suspect what would actually help her wipe her tears away, what would transform Rachel's sorrow into joy, would be if we actually did something more constructive. To be totally candid, I am not sure what it is we must do and where we should start. There are lots of opinions on this one, lots of exposed nerves. As we take a step forward, we must do so with great care and we must be forgiving if well-intentioned words cause unintended offense. But staying silent, avoiding the conversation – for those of us invested in the Jewish future, that simply cannot be an option. Let's do ourselves the dignity of being honest with ourselves and most importantly, honest and good to our daughters, our sons, and most of all, to the Jewish people.

Va-yiggash

The Blessing of Assimilation

The most interesting thing about the blessing one must recite upon seeing a king or secular head of state, is that such a blessing exists at all. *Barukh she-natan mik'vodo livriotav*. Blessed who gave of His glory to human beings." (Babylonian Talmud, Berachot 58a) I recited the blessing for the first time in my life this past Thursday as I stood in the presence of President Obama at the White House menorah lighting. The Hanukkah party was a who's who of the American Jewish community, a humbling and history-infused setting, and a great kiddush. I always knew there existed a blessing for such an occasion, but it was only when I actually recited it that I was struck by its curious nature. Why? Because, to state the obvious, the existence of a blessing presumes the possibility of those circumstances actually occurring. We have blessings for eating bread, for studying Torah, for seeing a crowd, for meeting a wise person, for bodily functions, for all sorts of things and occasions, all of which are likely to occur in a person's life. But to stand in the presence of a king or head of state? The fact that a minority and marginalized community of Talmudic rabbis bothered to codify such a blessing means one of two things. Either (a) they had an overblown estimation of their station in society or (b) there existed a statistical possibility that they would actually need to say such a blessing. In other words, what happened to me this past Thursday was not unheard of in Talmudic culture. And because it could, would, and continues to happen, thank goodness for the rabbis who ensured that we would have the just the right blessing to say in such an eventuality.

One need look no further than this week's parashah to see an early application of the blessing. I imagine the rabbis imagining Jacob reciting it as he arrives before the ruler of Egypt. "And Joseph brought his father Jacob and stood him before Pharaoh and Jacob blessed Pharaoh." (Genesis 47:7) On a textual level, the existence of the Talmudic *brakhah* answers the question of what Jacob actually may have said in that moment. But in sociological terms, embedded in the *brakhah* is an intriguing possibility regarding the posture of the Jewish world to secular culture. "Blessed is God who gave of His glory to His creatures," specifically, to non-Jews. Parochial as the Jewish community may have been, not only is contact with the non-Jewish world inevitable, not only is it not to be feared, but it is worthy of being blessed. God's glory is reserved neither for the heavens, nor for particular Jewish boundaries. God's glory embodied by non-Jews can redound back onto and strengthen the Jewish people, and is for that reason cause for appreciation and celebration.

This morning, I want to offer a contrarian sermon, a view that runs against the grain of much of what I have been reading (and sometimes saying) about the present and future condition of American Jewry. Typically, what we have been hearing is that the root cause of our waning numbers is our social and cultural engagement with secular society. That the story of American Jewry illustrates Salo Baron's aphorism that "what is good for Jews is not necessarily good for Judaism." Our engagement with non-Jews, our acceptance into secular society – these are the corrosive causes of our present troubles. The thinking that follows is that the only response to this slackening of Jewish identity is a Tevye-like cri-de-coeur for "Tradition!" It is time to circle the wagons. If we want a future, we have to turn inwards and turn back.

Given the luxury of speaking fairly regularly (and the ongoing high of the White House visit), I want to take a break from this "sky-is-falling," "woe-is-me" approach. This morning, I want to suggest that if we want to understand the historic secret to Jewish vitality, and thus mark out the path to securing a strong Jewish future, we will not find it by ignoring the non-Jewish world, but just the opposite, by engaging it – engaging it, adopting its qualities, and allowing Judaism to be strengthened because of that active and ongoing exchange.

Let me explain. In 1966, the late Chancellor of the Jewish Theological Seminary, Gerson D. Cohen, delivered a commencement address with the provocative title "The Blessing of Assimilation in Jewish History." While acknowledging the challenge of living in a free society, Cohen demonstrates as a historian that from the very first Jewish diaspora, the Jewish historical experience has been marked by an anxiety over assimilation coupled with a revitalization of Jewish life resulting from that very experience. On a cosmetic level, Cohen points out that famous Jewish names – like Aaron, Moses, Daniel, Zerubbabel, and Tryfon (or Tarfon) and so on – are not Jewish at all, but are all imports from the Egyptian, Babylonian, Hellenistic, and other communities in which Jews lived. We have always looked at and copied and adopted the dress and other practices of our non-Jewish neighbors. Just consider the black hats and coats of the present-day Hasidic community – garb that ironically is borrowed from seventeenth-century Polish gentry. More substantively, it was Jewish communities such as those in Alexandria and Cordoba, writing in Greek or Arabic, who were most effectively able to transmit our faith from generation to generation. But Cohen's argument goes even deeper. He explains that the Jewish cultural renaissance of Spain's Golden Age came by way of Arabic literary tastes; the Mussar/pietist movement of French and German Jewry developed due to a familiarity with Christian theology; and Hasidic mystical doctrines evince an ongoing acquaintance with Sufi doctrine. To put it another way, the greatest, most enduring, and most vital periods of Jewish life and living – the emergence of the Kabbalah, the philosophy of Maimonides, to name only two – happened not by the Jews withdrawing from non-Jewish life, but by assimilating non-Jewish life into Judaism and thus enabling Judaism to be transformed and revitalized. As David Ruderman of the University of Pennsylvania argues in his recent book on early modern Jewry, there exists a causal relationship between Jewish mobility and cultural production. We arrive in a new place, we appreciate and absorb the blessings of that world, and we are rendered a stronger Jewish community because of that encounter. In Cohen's own words, "Assimilation properly channeled and exploited *can* be a blessing." (*Jewish History and Jewish Destiny*, p. 155)

As interesting as the historical reflections may be, the question for us is not merely descriptive, but prescriptive: To what degree does this hold true for us today? If we take a look at American Jewry, we easily see the pattern continuing. What are our synagogues, federations, and JCCs if not communal structures modeled after those of our Protestant hosts? The philosophy of Mordecai Kaplan – modeled after that of John Dewey. The music of Debbie Friedman, Shlomo Carlebach, Meir Finkelstein and so many others – all given life by the American musical traditions from which they emerge. Jewish scholarship and Jewish journals written in English – modeled after their secular counterparts. Nice Jewish kids with names like Lucy, Maddie, Zoe, and Jed. Unpack a whole lot of what is great about Jewish life, and you will inevitably find non-Jewish ideas, themes and social structures. The efflorescence of American Jewry may be explained precisely by our conscious and unconscious assimilation of secular categories of thinking into Jewish ones.

As Cohen himself points out, as long as Jews live in a non-Jewish world, such an exchange is inevitable. The difference between whether it is a good thing, a cross-fertilization and revitalization, or a bad thing, a slackening of Jewish identity, comes down to the question of whether non-Jewish forms of expression are assimilated into Jewish life, or Jewish life and Jews are assimilated into non-Jewish life. The great cultural Zionist Ahad Ha'am coined the term *ḥikkui shel hitḥarut*, "competitive imitation," to describe the process whereby cultural traditions influence and impact each other in reciprocal ways. The key is that that the communities in question must be strong and vital unto themselves for the exchange to be mutually enriching. To have it otherwise, to have a weak Jewish culture in the tidal wave of America, will ultimately result not in imitation but in assimilation.

Lest there be any doubt, I think that this is exactly the conversation that we, as a Conservative synagogue committed to *both* tradition *and* change, should be modeling. Whether it is the melody of *L'kha Dodi*, the manner in which our children are educated, or the social media platforms by which we communicate with each other, we are obligated to engage in and often imitate the cultural milieu in which we exist. If it is our goal, which I think it is, to make Judaism accessible and relevant to the lives of American Jews, then both the "what" and the "how" of what we do here needs to reflect that goal. And yet, we also need to remember the distinctive rituals, themes, and values of our people that make a Jewish way of life worth preserving in the first place. The hope is not to produce some sort of queer "menurkey"-like Judaism that succeeds neither in loyalty to our spiritual inheritance, nor in accommodation to our present-day context. If nothing else, we should remember that there is something delightfully countercultural about being Jewish, and we must be just as attentive to retaining our points of distinction as to assimilating the blessings of the world in which we live.

As I indicated before, our parashah chronicles the migration of our people into the first Jewish diaspora. Upon hearing that his son Joseph was still alive, Jacob, along with his entire household, journeys from the Promised Land down towards Egypt. For the final time, Jacob sets camp, and filled with anxiety and fear, has a nighttime vision. What exactly, the commentators ask, was Jacob afraid of? He was, after all, on his way to be reunited with his beloved Joseph. The nineteenth-century commentator Naftali Tzvi Yehuda of Berlin, the Netziv, explains that Jacob feared that "his seed would be absorbed by the Egyptian nation." God's message to Jacob "Fear not . . . for I will make you a great nation," signals God's assurance that this diaspora would not be the end of the Jewish people, but an opportunity to become a great a populous nation, a *goy gadol*. This is the first, but not the last time the Jewish people will move from one place to another, expressing anxiety that such a move will result in a diminution of Jewish identity. Jewish renewal doesn't happen all by itself. It takes intentional leadership, and it means making tough choices. But secular culture unto itself need not be the source of fear; time and again it has proven to be an opportunity for growth and transformation. Like Jacob himself standing before Pharaoh, we can allow for the possibility that it is even deserving of our gratitude and our blessing.

Va-y'ḥi

The Greater Good

J ews don't believe in the Christian concept of original sin, but if we did, our tainted condition would result from a sin that occurred towards the end of the book of Genesis, not the beginning. "Because they sold a *tzaddik* (a righteous person) for silver," explains the book of Amos, God's wrath was provoked. (2:6) Jacob's sons selling their brother Joseph to the Egypt-bound caravan was and would remain the foundational transgression of our people. According to the apocryphal Book of Jubilees, the sale of Joseph into servitude occurred on the tenth day of the seventh month, corresponding to what we know today as Yom Kippur. Ever since that fateful day described in the book of Genesis, it has been ordained that the children of Israel should afflict themselves, gathering each year to make atonement, seeking to cleanse themselves of an intergenerational wrong that we just can't shake. Explicitly and implicitly we re-enact the contours of the crime. Every Yom Kippur we read about the sending of the goat bearing the people's sins out into the wilderness, like Joseph. Every Yom Kippur afternoon, we recite the Martyrology, the account of the sacrifice of the ten martyrs, sentenced to death, according to tradition, for the sin of the ten brothers. The fraternal strife of the sons of Jacob sits at the fault line of our people.

All of which begs the following question: What caused one brother to sell another into slavery in the first place? What was so terrible as to prompt such an egregious act, one that would not only split the first family of our people but have a ripple effect in the generations to follow? If I had to put my finger on it, I would say it was the inability of the brothers, Joseph included, to let the greater good prevail over their respective shortcomings. The tragedy of the sons of Jacob was that despite being born of the same father, raised in the same household, these siblings chose to inflate their differences at the expense of *shalom bayit*, peace in the home. Every party was to blame. "And Joseph brought bad reports of [his brothers] to [Jacob]," a busybody youth who had no discretion. As for the brothers, they saw Jacob's favoritism, made explicit by the coat of many colors draped on Joseph, and "they could not speak a peaceable word to him." Was it right for Jacob to favor Joseph? Of course not. Were the brothers a bunch of choirboys? I doubt it. The first family of the Jewish people had more than its fair share of subplots and palace intrigue. On countless occasions Joseph should have held his tongue and demonstrated the maturity not to speak his mind. But the brothers for their part proved unable to see past his childish behavior. Are we really to believe that they had no other option than to conspire to kill their own flesh and blood? It was Sigmund Freud who coined the term "the narcissism of minor differences," the notion that it is more often than not the minor differences, not the major ones, that are the source of strife between people. It is precisely the little things that ultimately caused the unraveling of the house of Jacob.

If the rift between Joseph and his siblings stems from this shortcoming, then it is only with its rectification and redress that their relationship is mended. Ostensibly, their reconciliation happened last week as Joseph finally revealed himself to his brothers. But what the reader knows, what the rabbis intuited, and what the brothers no doubt well understood, was that last week's revelation was not necessarily prompted by a spirit of forgiveness, but by Joseph's concern for his father Jacob's well-being and Joseph's desire to see him. Why else would the first words Joseph blurts out to his brothers be "I am Joseph. Is my father alive?!" Arguably, Joseph's primary concern in last week's dénouement was not his relationship with his brothers, not coming to terms with his past, but a desire to be reunited with his father.

All of which is a roundabout way of saying that this week's Torah reading is really, really important. Because only this week do we see how the siblings interact once their father Jacob has died. On a side note, this is a topic that I could write volumes about from a pastoral perspective: the fascinating and tortured and sometimes liberating dynamic that takes place among children when they are called on to recalibrate their relationships upon the death of a parent. In the case of Jacob's children, we cannot be sure whether the children's previous actions were motivated by their own feelings or out of deference to their father. Nevertheless, collectively they fulfill Jacob's dying wish; the siblings carry their father back to the land of Canaan for proper burial. The midrash explains that as they began their return trip back down to Egypt, the procession passed by the very pit into which Joseph had been thrown some decades before. Joseph's reaction, not surprisingly, is very different from that of the brothers but also different from that which you might have expected. The midrash explains that Joseph stared into the pit, reflected on the serendipitous journey of his life, and recited a blessing expressing gratitude to God for having performed miracles for him and bestowing upon him so much good. The brothers, however, see Joseph peering into the pit into which they had thrown him, are reminded of their initial offense, and with their father now dead, fear for their lives, believing Joseph will finally exact his revenge. Only at this point, when the brothers relay a fabricated deathbed request by Jacob that Joseph should forgive them, does Joseph respond with a magnanimous spirit of forgiveness that we know is truly his.

If, as Maimonides teaches, the litmus test for a true penitent is when a person has the ability to commit the same transgression but chooses not to, then the correlative principle must be true as well. How did Joseph know, how do any of us know, when we have truly forgiven someone for a wrong committed against us? At the moment that we have the capacity to do exactly the same thing to a person as that person did to us, but we choose not to do it. Joseph meets this test and then some. "Have no fear" he tells his brothers, ". . . For while you intended me harm, God intended it for good, to bring about the present result." As Dr. Avivah Zornberg points out in her study of the scene, Joseph was able to leverage his pain into hope and reconciliation. I imagine it was at this moment that Joseph took a deep breath, or more likely two or three, mulled over whether to quibble about the truth and thus push the squabble forward or take the high road, give his brothers a pass, and get on with the business of living. We know it is exactly this latter path that he decides to take. The youthful Joseph would never have let it slide. It is not exactly clear just how close Joseph and the brothers would be in the years ahead; the text does not provide detail. All we do know is that it is only here and now, after their father died, that we can assess the brothers' relationship on it its own terms. It is only here that we know, once and for all, that the minor differences dividing the brothers melt away in the warm radiant glow of the greater good.

Today we say goodbye to the Joseph story, not to be engaged with it again for just under a year – or at the earliest, next Yom Kippur, depending on how you look at it. I suspect however, that its lessons will resonate year-round because it is the story not only of the first family of our people but of all our families. Brothers and sisters, family and friends who have every reason to see the greater good, to work for *shalom bayit*, but who – because we are still wired, well, like our predecessors – wake up to relationships that are frayed for reasons that we can't quite explain, never mind defend. Far too often, far too many of us fail to see the greater good. Our minor grievances eclipse a relationship, our focus is petty, and the richness of our lives is diminished. As noted many times in the past week, it was Nelson Mandela who famously explained that "Resentment is like drinking a poison and then hoping it will kill your enemies." Unlike Mandela's case, the pedestrian grudges we bear separate us for the most part not from enemies but from family and would-be friends. As Ben Zoma taught in *Pirkei Avot* (4:1), might is not measured in physical strength, but in our ability to conquer our inclinations – not an easy task by any stretch, but necessary if we want our relationships to endure beyond inevitable stumbles.

Cain and Abel, Isaac and Ishmael, Jacob and Esau, Joseph and his brothers – the families of the book of Genesis cut so close to home because in many ways their internal dynamics reflect our own. Which is why it makes so much sense that the blessing we bestow on our families every Friday night comes from this week's parashah. "May God make you like Ephraim and Manasseh." The two brothers Ephraim and Manasseh, Joseph's children and Jacob's grandchildren, hold a distinction that sets them apart, not just from their predecessors, but also from families yet to come. *They got along peaceably with one another.* They were the first biblical siblings who didn't let strife and pettiness mar their lives. At my Shabbos table, at your Shabbos table, in all our homes, it is our hope and aspiration for our children to be like Ephraim and Manasseh. If we want it to happen, it will take more than just a blessing. It will take hard work, an expansion of our souls, and most of all, a willingness to see past pettiness and difference. Not easy, but given what is at stake, well worth the effort.

Sh'mot

The Counterfactual

Down the rabbit hole I fell this past Monday, faster and further than I had ever imagined possible. I had been invited to present a paper at the AJS conference in Boston, the annual gathering of the Association of Jewish Studies, comprised of Jewish studies academics from around the world. I wasn't due to speak until the afternoon, which gave me the day to sit in on other presenters – top professors and up-and-coming scholars, each one smarter than the next. No question, the currency of academic conferences is erudition, with more fifty-cent words than this Big Ten graduate ever imagined possible. Deconstructionism, structuralism, post-modernism, signifiers and signified, Derrida, Habermas, Ricoeur, Saussure – all sorts of tortured words and name dropping in order to package ideas with an air of depth, profundity, and originality. More than once as I listened to the presenters, I recalled the line from Gilbert and Sullivan, "If this young man expresses himself in terms too deep for me, why, what a very singularly deep young man this deep young man must be!" There were sessions on "Jewish and Post-Colonial Thought," on "Pre-Modern Jewish Texts Post-Kant," on "Urban Transformations and Associational Life in Istanbul, Izmir, and Salonica." Never before had I heard so many Jews talk about so many Jewish things without a single Goldstein joke (though there was a paper on Jacobson's *The Finkler Question*).

Rock bottom was probably Session 4.1, "Counterfactualism and Jewish History." Four papers by four different professors of fairly significant stature all speaking on the subject of a series of "what ifs" in Jewish history. "What if a bi-national state had arisen in Palestine?" "What if Arabs had been willing to compromise before 1948?" "What if Franz Kafka had immigrated to Palestine?" The first thought I had in my mind as I sat down in the session (after registering regret at not taking an aisle seat) was that these people have way too much time on their hands. I mean, it is one thing for historians to discuss the particulars of what happened in the past, another thing for them to debate the question of what these past events do or don't mean. But to convene a conversation so they could speculate on a past that never actually happened? Really? For this your parents took out loans to send you to college and graduate school?

But with nowhere to go and a speaker still yet to speak, I decided to make lemons into lemonade, and my thoughts and laptop turned to a far more practical and timely question than the meta-historical and non-directional discourse in which I was stuck. The question that is always on my mind: "Is there any way I can use this towards a good sermon?" And while I have no doubt that you will share the answer to this question with me in a forthright manner at kiddush, in the intimacy of this late December Shabbat, I ask for your patience and indulgence as I try to state my case.

Knowingly or not, each of us has crafted and carries around a self-narrative. It is altogether natural and understandable to do so. We were each born into a set of circumstances, and either by nature or nurture, happenstance, or steadily pursued design, the pathway of our life and shape of our character emerged. And we tell that story to ourselves and to each other in order to explain who we are today. To use an easy example: me. I am the grandson of a congregational rabbi, I grew up in a traditional Jewish household, one of four children. I fell under the mentorship of a charismatic Hillel director, met a beautiful Jewish girl during a post-college year in Israel and poof! Here I am today: father of four, rabbi of a large synagogue composed of roughly the same demographic as my home community, in a similar urban setting – the one difference being the superior West Coast weather of my youth. There is coherence, there is causality, and there is an air of inevitability to the story. What is true for our personal histories is also true for the narratives on the world stage. We know how the story ends, the Great Depression, the fall of the Berlin Wall, the Second Intifada. There is, to adopt the title of Michael André Bernstein's book on the subject, a "foregone conclusion." With the finale at hand, it is just a matter of engaging in the process of "backshadowing," in other words, reconstructing the turn of events in order to arrive at the predetermined goal. Or if you want to use a big word to say the same thing, a teleological telling of history, history told with the end in mind.

While there is nothing terribly wrong with writing history this way – it is actually the way most histories are told – a bit of caution is also in order. Because whether it is the events of our lives or those on the world stage, there is a pitfall in recitations of the past that are too tight, too coherent, and too inevitable. Why? Because if you understand your present as somehow predetermined, then you are also rendering human creativity and freedom irrelevant. (Bernstein, *Foregone Conclusions*, p. 28) If your past is understood as the necessary and only prologue to your present, if you believe all outcomes to be pre-ordained, then you risk abdicating responsibility for the millions of decisions that you actually made in order to arrive at the present. Nothing in this world just happens, nobody stands at their position in life without having encountered the prospect and possibility of very different outcomes. We make choices at every turn that need to be acknowledged, understood, and owned. It is much tidier to believe that everything worked out as it was meant to be, that it could not have been otherwise, but that is hardly a mindset that will lead to a responsible and accountable life. Take, for example, the Giants season. I guarantee that at the end of the year, when the NFL shows the Giants' "season in review," the story will be told as if their collapse was inevitable. But you and I all know that it was far from a foregone conclusion that a quarterback with two Super Bowl rings would throw a career record of interceptions, that unforeseen injuries to both running backs would cripple the Giants' ability to run the ball and control the clock, and that a team of veteran players would inexplicably get old overnight. The season didn't have to turn out this way, but it did for a variety of reasons, some in the Giants' control and some not. But it was by no means inevitable. History can be told by way of "backshadowing," but for those interested in an accountable life, in shaping the present and future, far more productive is the act of what Bernstein calls "side shadowing," seeing the world as it could have been, the counterfactual, the roads not taken. Only at the moment that we stand squarely and reflect on what might have been, what could have happened, is there a possibility for what is called human agency, the foundational and fundamental embrace of our ability to make choices, to own our decisions and thus be full participants, not just spectators, in the unfolding narratives of our lives.

This is exactly what happens to Moses in this week's parashah. If there was ever a person who could not claim credit for the circumstances of his existence, it was Moses. Saved from Pharaoh's decree by being hidden in a reed basket on the Nile, rescued by Pharaoh's daughter, raised in an environment of royalty and distinction – given the blessings of his life, Moses could have gone on to live a carefree life of entitlement. In fact, Moses had every reason, as Joseph did, to see his elevated station in Egyptian society as some sort of expression of manifest destiny. But then, in the critical scene that would make Moses Moses, the text states: "And Moses grew up and went out to see his brethren and he saw their burdens." (Exodus 2:11) If this were a movie, it would be precisely here that the director would replay all the points of Moses' life that led to this moment. Only here does it register for Moses that at each of these points, things could have turned out very differently. And then, flashing back to the present, Moses sees the Egyptian striking his Hebrew brother and Moses defends the Hebrew. Only here, only now, when Moses engages the counterfactual of his life – that he could have been and should have been either a Hebrew slave, or more likely, dead – does he do what he has not done before: He steps up. He takes ownership and responsibility for who he is. He may have always known he was a Hebrew, but only here does it click in his mind that the combination of his tribal identity and his Egyptian upbringing positions him for a unique leadership role. It doesn't happen overnight; he still runs away and then argues with God at the Burning Bush. But it is only now, when Moses sees his brethren and acknowledges that his own circumstances could have been and should have been otherwise, that he asserts himself into the narrative of his life. Only now does he appreciate his blessings, and more importantly, embrace the role he has to play.

Our lives are not the stuff of sacred scripture. Depending on who you are and the mood you are in, you may have arrived today believing yourself to have a particularly good, or bad, lot in life. In our jobs, our marriages, our families, our quiet needs by "sun and candle-light," it is natural and understandable to construct self-narratives with an air of inevitability. We shrug our shoulders, mind our business, accept our challenges and blessings, and resign ourselves to lead lives of either quiet desperation or inconsequential entitlement. But the thing is, our lives *could* have been different, and while that may be unnerving, it also means our lives *can* be different and *that* is thrilling.

What hit me most about going to the AJS conference was that for me, the entire experience was a voyeuristic journey into a world that could have been. There was a time, as some of you may know, that I was a doctoral student at University of Chicago looking forward to a career in academia. On Monday, I saw former classmates, my would-have-been colleagues; I stepped into a world that was once mine and it was, I can't lie, an exquisite feeling. During my presentation, everyone referred to me as Dr. Cosgrove, a title that I have not heard for years. There was a siren call, an allure, no question, to the road not travelled. But then something happened. I was sitting in a session, trying to listen intently to two scholars parse out a hair-splitting philosophical difference between Gersonides and Maimonides on providential design, and all of a sudden I heard myself say a little too loud under my breath, "I'm good." "I'm good worrying about the Schwartz bar mitzvah dates. I'm good worrying about what kind of cookies we serve at kiddush and what constitutes a nut-free environment. I'm good wondering whether we made the Kol Nidre numbers and whether the kids I bar mitzvahed do or don't get into college. I am good serving the pastoral needs of my community, going to staff meetings with great colleagues, preaching every week, and seeing my community grow. I am also – I think – good at it. And most importantly, I am grateful. In fact, exactly at that moment, I realized I felt much better than good, I felt great. Like that Rupert Holmes song, having looked around, I came to realize that what I really wanted was actually exactly what I had all along. I stood toe-to-toe with my counterfactual and I got on that train to New York "back to auld claes and porridge," and you know what, I have been flying ever since.

If the book of Exodus is about anything, it is about liberation from slavery. But you and I know that servitude comes in many forms, sometimes physical, but often spiritual. And sometimes, the source of our oppression comes from the most unexpected place – ourselves. A dip into the road not traveled keeps us alert to the fact that every second of our lives is a turning point. Our lives up until now were not predetermined; it could have been otherwise and there are an infinite number of reasons why it isn't. Like Moses himself, we can leverage this awareness to acknowledge the gift of our portion, *yismaḥ Moshe b'matnat ḥelko*, and more importantly as free men and women, we can act in control of our destiny. *Ehyeh asher ehyeh*, I will be that which I will be. Always in the process of becoming, always owning our decisions, and always players on the stage of the story of our lives.

B'shallaḥ
'Who is a Jew?' Revisited

Generations from now, when the history of American Jewry is produced – please God even as new chapters are still being written – there will be a footnote, if not an entire chapter, on Adam Sandler. One cold December night some twenty years ago, in the midst of an otherwise forgettable *Saturday Night Live* "Weekend Update," this often funny and frequently crude comedian sang what would become an anthem for American Jewry. Calling it the "Hanukkah Song," with nearly every line rhyming with "harmonica" or "Veronica," Sandler sang the Rolodex of Jewish American celebrity. In his words: "David Lee Roth lights the Menorah, so do James Caan, Kirk Douglas and the late Dinah Shore-ah." My favorite stanza:

> Guess who eats together at the Carnegie Deli,
> Bowzer from Sha Na Na and Arthur Fonzerelli.
> Paul Newman's half-Jewish, Goldie Hawn's half, too.
> Put them together, what a fine lookin' Jew.

I remember laughing very hard the first time I heard it, and more recently, experiencing wistful nostalgia as Debbie and I realized that our children didn't know a single name listed.

Twenty years later, I would contend that the song is not just a cultural marker in my own life, but a turning point in the American Jewish condition. Why? Because it was on that night that the genie was let out of the bottle on the age-old question of "Who is a Jew?" The novelty of the song was not the public, pride-filled, and tongue-in-cheek embrace by a Jewish comic of his or her Jewish identity; Woody Allen, Mel Brooks, Gilda Radner, and too many others to mention had done that before. What made the skit notable was that Sandler exposed the democratic and slippery and prickly nature of American Jewish identity. Harrison Ford, Rod Carew, and all Three Stooges, by birth or by conversion, matrilineal or patrilineal, true or not true – that night the boundaries of Jewish identity became a lot more porous. Being a "Jew" was a label that could be assigned or acquired by the authority of . . . Adam Sandler. A Wild West opened up, where to be a "Jew," one merely needed to act or be perceived to be "Jew-ish," and it was so and nobody could say otherwise.

The opening chapter of Professor Shaul Magid's recent book on American Jewry is titled "Be the Jew You Make: Jews, Judaism and Jew-ishness in Post-ethnic America." (*American Post-Judaism*, 2013) The take-home message, as you may guess, is one and the same as that of the Adam Sandler song. Not just Jews, but all of America, Magid explains, has become post-ethnic. He means that it is no longer the case that blood, or history, or memory determines identity. It is the voluntary affiliations, not the involuntary ones, that now make people who they are. There may have been a time when who your grandparents were determined who you are, but as Magid points out, you need look no further than the mixed-racial parentage of our President to know that the ironclad assumptions of that era are no longer operative. In a sentence, America is no longer a society founded on "descent," but one founded by "consent." If we feel Jewish, or if Adam Sandler thinks or says we are, then that makes it so. In Magid's words, "religion is increasingly a product of voluntarism and inventiveness as opposed to inherited tradition." (p. 19) Or, as the title of another survey of American Jewry puts it: "'Grande Soy Vanilla Latte with Cinnamon, No Foam' . . . Jewish Identity and Community in a Time of Unlimited Choices." (Bennett, et. al. *Reboot*, 2006)

Depending on who you are, you may believe these developments to be a good thing or a bad thing. On the one hand, with a looser definition of "Who is a Jew?" there could be more and more people who find themselves identifying with our people. How amazing is it that we live in a time that people just want to be Jewish! On the other hand, many may argue, there is a consequence to all this: a cheapening of what it means to be a Jew, theologically, historically, communally and otherwise. After all, if everyone who wants to be a Jew can do so simply by asserting it to be the case, then at what point does that claim become meaningless? As Americans we shudder at the thought of anyone telling us who we can and can't say we are. But as Jews we know that the situation is a bit more textured. At the very least, when it comes to matters of personal identity, just because you say it, doesn't make it so.

What we can all agree on is – or at least all the data seems to indicate – that we are entering, if not already living in, a new chapter of American Jewish life. One of the most fascinating byproducts of the recent studies of New York and American Jewry is the new glossary of terms in use. It used to be that Jews were Orthodox, Conservative, Reform, Ashkenazic, Sephardic, a few atheists, and Madeleine Albright. Now there are Jews of no religion, Jews by personal decision, partial Jews, and more. Some of these people may have a Madonna-like affection for Jewish mysticism, some may just have an ex-spouse who was Jewish, and some just say they feel at home in the faith. The sociologist Steven Cohen calls these Jews with melded or malleable or fluid identities "borderland Jews." They have liminal identities. Some practice other faiths; some do not. There is a statistically significant and growing number of people who are, for lack of a better word, Jews by cultural affinity. Proud and self-confident, not Jewish by any halakhic (Jewish legal) definition, but laying claim as stakeholders in our people's destiny.

To make matters even more complicated, and for reasons we can delve into another day, the exact opposite trend is taking place in Israel. The Israeli Chief Rabbinate is rapidly moving to constrict the definition of who is a Jew and who is authorized to vouch for someone's Jewishness. As you may know, because of the manner in which Israeli society is structured, all matters of personal status (birth, marriage, conversion, burial) are under the authority of the Chief Rabbinate. So, for instance, when two Jews from the Diaspora register to get married in Israel, the Israeli rabbinate requires some sort of letter vouching for the Jewishness of the individuals in question. You may have read of the firestorm that erupted this past week as the bona fides of mainstream Orthodox rabbis have been rejected by an increasingly insular Israeli Chief Rabbinate. In the eyes of the State of Israel, American Jews are no longer empowered to say "who is a Jew." It is a terrible turn of events, a state of affairs whose only silver lining is that the American Orthodox rabbinate finally understands what Conservative and Reform rabbis have been complaining about all these years. In other words, a perfect storm has emerged between the two centers of the Jewish world, America and Israel. A loosening definition of Jewish identity in America and a tightening in Israel – both problematic, probably interrelated, and together, with potentially calamitous consequences. One Jewry watered down beyond recognition and the other parochialized beyond relevance at its own peril. Neither one interested in acknowledging the other, neither one invested in the other's well-being. The prophet Jeremiah prophesied that the destroyers of the Jewish people will come from within. We are a small enough people with big enough problems as it is, and here we are tearing each other apart from the inside with nobody to blame but ourselves.

So what is the answer? It is a good question and – as a congregation that is both traditional and liberal in its sensibilities – we can take some leadership in responding. I do take some solace in the knowledge that the problem at hand is not entirely unprecedented. As early as in the events of this week's parashah, the emancipated Israelites experienced a redefinition of identity upon entering a new chapter of wilderness existence with nobody but themselves who would tell them who they were. Liberated from Egyptian bondage, they sang a triumphant song as they passed safely through the Sea of Reeds. "This is my God and I will glorify Him; My father's God, and I will exalt Him." (Exodus 15:2) At one and the same time, they asserted a voluntary, intimate, and personal relationship with their faith – "This is my God" – and laid claim to the faith of their predecessors – "My father's God, and I will exalt Him." Neither one by itself was sufficient. As free Jews, the Israelites insisted on establishing a relationship with God on their own terms, in the coin of their day. Yet they also were able to understand that personal religious experience as connected to their ancestral faith. That they could see it as one and the same project – that realization, as much as the theatrics of splitting the sea – was the miracle of our parashah.

There are those in the Jewish world who believe that the only response to the emergent Jewish demography is to circle the wagons. And there are those who believe that the first and only loyalty of Judaism is to Jews; Judaism is whatever Jews say it is – no matter who says it and how that Judaism is expressed. Here in this sanctuary, we reject the premise that it is an either/or proposition. Ours must be a Judaism of both descent and consent: "The God of my fathers" and "My God." In the words of my teacher Louis Jacobs, "Both concepts are essential to Jewish piety, the one giving strength to the other." (*We Have Reason to Believe*, p. 32) We stand on new shores, facing a wilderness, a Wild West that we are still seeking to understand. No matter what course we choose, the condition of the Jewish people as a whole must always be of paramount importance. In North America, in Israel – and most of all – between the two. A shared Jewish destiny linked together in space and in time: past, present and – most of all – future.

Something to Talk About

It is not often that the line at the salad bar launches a sermon – but for the purposes of this morning I need to set the scene. It was just about two weeks ago that I was standing in line at the salad bar in an all-inclusive holiday resort in the Dominican Republic when a bathing suit clad man in front of me bellowed at his son, *Yuval, atah ḥonek et ha-tur*, "Yuval, you are holding up the line." We have all been in the situation before; on vacation or traveling abroad we overhear a bit of Hebrew: the discovery of a surreptitious Israeli in our midst. Whether we speak a lot of Hebrew, or not very much at all, the Israeli's linguistic "tell" triggers a sense of kinship in the Diaspora Jew. Who knew? Right here in the Dominican Republic! My daughter looked up at me smiling. She knew that we knew what he didn't know yet – that we all belong to the same people. I am a friendly guy, he seemed to be a friendly guy. His children were bugging him, my children bug me. Neither of us had anywhere to go other than our beach chairs. Why not strike up a conversation with my Israeli kinsman?

The most interesting part about the whole incident, what I want to talk to you about this morning, is not what happened, but rather what didn't happen. Despite the incredibly low barrier of entry for sociability, despite all the reasons to do or say something, the truth is I did and said absolutely nothing. We stood there next to each other in line, the moment passed, and life continued as normal. He never knew that I knew. For him there was no incident to reflect on. As for me, as you can tell, I have thought about it often, about the conversation that never occurred.

I am deeply worried that American Jews and secular Israelis have nothing to talk about. I can speak a fumbling Hebrew, I have visited Israel more times than I can count, even lived there for extended periods. I privately and publicly advocate on Israel's behalf and, by dint of my day job, can pick up the phone and call or exchange emails with a number of not insignificant representatives of the Jewish state. But put me in a bathing suit and stand me next to a 40-something secular Israeli, and I am not exactly sure what we have in common beyond watching our receding hairlines and cholesterol levels. What exactly is the Jewish conversation that I can engage him in? Are you interested in who will be the next head of UJA? Do you even know what UJA is? What about the future of Conservative Judaism? Have you read the Pew study, or even this week's parashah? Even were we to talk about Israel, I wonder if we would have anything to say? Do you follow what is happening on college campuses regarding the Israeli-Palestinian dialogue? Are you concerned that American academic associations are boycotting Israeli academics? Do you care that I care about religious pluralism and Women of the Wall? Are any of your concerns mine? Or mine yours? Besides, had I "outed" myself as a Jew that day standing in line, would you feel any kinship? How do you – if you do at all – connect to the global Jewish people? I get it. You speak fluent Hebrew, served in the Israeli army, and fulfilled the mitzvah of living in the land of Israel – no small things. But you don't go to synagogue, aren't involved in Jewish communal life, and show no indication of being a stakeholder in Diaspora Jewry. And while I work hard to support you politically and economically, to the best that I can tell, were North American Jewry, God forbid, to melt away like the polar ice cap, you would continue to go about your business as if nothing had happened. Despite my tone, my point is not to make judgments. God bless secular Israelis, especially the atheists. I am simply trying to paint the demographic situation as I see it. Six million Jews here, six million Jews there; many of the Israelis are secular. None of us really have much to say to each other as Jews.

In order to understand how we got here, I need to pull the camera back to a wide angle, both philosophically and historically. First, philosophically. Precisely eighty years ago, Rabbi Mordecai Kaplan stated a thesis in a now-famous book called *Judaism as a Civilization*. He wasn't the first to state this thesis, but he said it best and said it often, and so we think of him when we cite it. Kaplan contended that Judaism takes shape according to the context in which it functions. Jewish ritual, theology, music, group identity – everything – is informed by the Jewish community practicing that Judaism. And Jews, necessarily, are products of the time and place in which they live. So the Judaism of Alexandrian Jewry was different from the Judaism of the Middle Ages, different from that of the Spanish Golden Age, eighteenth-century Ashkenaz, twentieth-century Iraq and so on and so forth. All these Jews were Jewish, but their "Judaisms" looked very different, because they functioned in different contexts. The soil if you will, in which the Jewish *neshamah* took root, inevitably nurtured and determined the Jewish expression that blossomed.

The thesis is clear, pretty straightforward, and even a bit obvious, but you can see why it is important in order to understand me and my proverbial (or actual) Israeli counterpart. We are both Jews, but I have grown up in this place called America and he in Israel and so naturally – our "Judaisms" will be very different.

Here is where it gets very interesting – and historical. My new friend and colleague Dr. Einat Wilf recently brought to my attention some articles by Dr. Shlomo Fischer of the Jewish People Policy Institute. (blogs.timesofisrael.com/author/shlomo-fischer/) Dr. Fischer explains that ever since the Pilgrims came to America in search of religious freedom, America's DNA has encouraged the ideals of freedom of expression and religious pluralism. With the exception of a few Tea Party types, the Protestant brand of American religion, for the most part, has understood that while religious values may or even must inform the public square (think Martin Luther King, Jr.), the separation of church and state ensures that Catholic or Jew, majority or minority, all of us, may practice our faith in any way we choose, if we choose to do so at all. From this American soil grew American Orthodox, Conservative, Reform, Reconstructionist, and Renewal, Jubus, Debbie Friedman Jews, Carlebach Jews, all sorts of Jews. The promise of America is the promise that you can practice your Judaism as you see fit. In fact, as Americans we will "go to the mat" to protect that very right.

The forces that shaped Jewish life in Israel could not have been more different. First of all, we need to remember that at its core, political Zionism was a secular answer to the problem of being a Jew in the modern world. The secular Zionism of Theodore Herzl, though it was a fulfillment of a multi-millennial Jewish longing, was also a rupture with everything that came before. Israel meant that a Jew could be a Jew without being "Jew-ish," a national identity replacing a religious one. Were there religious Zionists? Of course there were. Lots of them. But in many respects, the establishment of the State of Israel was a rejection of the Diaspora religious Jew. In a story told in many histories of Israel, for reasons of political expediency, at the founding of the State, Ben-Gurion farmed out the religious ministries to a chief rabbinate whose religious sensibility represented neither his own nor that of the vast majority of Israeli society. Ever since, according to Fischer, for secular Israelis, the chief rabbinate and its functionaries are there merely to provide *sherutei dat,* "religious services" – public utilities supported by taxes akin to the electric or gas company. "Let them," the thinking goes, "officiate at the wedding or funeral; then give the rabbi a tip and file it away as an annoyance equal to paying the public television tax." The point is that your typical secular Israeli neither cares about the chief rabbinate, nor for that matter, understands why Diaspora Jews are so upset about it. They just want to get on with living their lives; that was, after all, the whole point of Zionism in the first place.

To put it even more provocatively, according to this line of thinking, even suggesting that the Judaism of American Jews and that of secular Israelis are *drifting apart* is going one step too far. Secular Israelis may be Jewish in a technical sense, but their identities are national, not religious. I am not sure if I totally agree, but it does explain why when secular Israelis leave Israel they don't understand or associate with conventional expressions of Diaspora Jewish life. Sometimes they walk into my office when they fall in love with a non-Jew, but for the most part, aside from bumping into us in the East Village or at a David Broza concert at the 92nd Street Y, secular Israelis in the Diaspora are totally disconnected from American Judaism. My Jewish concerns are not their concerns, nor are theirs mine. There was a time that we shared the responsibility to memorialize the Shoah, but that memory has been internalized differently by us, and with every passing year, recedes as a common point of reference.

Lest American Jews think we get a free pass, there is much soul-searching we need to do. Going to an AIPAC or J Street convention, important as it is – and it is – is for far too many a compensatory act to make up for not having an actual relationship with Israelis or a substantive Jewish identity. *Start-up Nation* may be a terrific a book, but there is something terribly wrong if we think focusing on Israel's hi-tech industry is an act of Jewish identity building. Downloading Waze onto your iPhone because it is an Israeli start-up doth not ensure Jewish continuity! Somewhere along the way, American Jews have come to believe that their important and often critical work on behalf of Israel is the same as having relationships with Israelis or, even worse, with Judaism itself.

And so we are back to where we started: American Jews and secular Israelis with nothing to say to one another. If you are wondering why I am leaving religious Israelis out of it, it is because I picked on them last week. But just because we are eyes wide open to the Jewish world as it is, doesn't mean we should, for one second, abdicate our commitment to the Jewish world as it *ought* to be. Any vision of a robust Jewish peoplehood must include a dialogue between the two major centers of the Jewish people. We can and should continue to send as many people to Israel as possible, young and old, and Israelis can and should create similar opportunities to engage with and understand Diaspora Jewry. Bridges must be built, new Birthrights imagined, exchanges and cultural projects undertaken. In an Internet/Skype era there is no excuse not to have dialogue. Locally, there is so much we can do. We talk all the time about outreach to the unaffiliated. You would think that a synagogue with an Israeli ḥazzan might come up with one or two ideas to tap into the reservoir of Israeli expats running around New York City. How amazing would it be if Park Avenue Synagogue didn't just have an interfaith trialogue with Muslims and Christians, but also had an "intra-Jewish dialogue" with Israelis living in New York City? There is so much we can do, so many ways to build bridges, and so few reasons why we wouldn't at least give it a try.

The first, and for that matter, the only time Jewish identity took expression in a vacuum was in this week's parashah, when the Torah was given at Mount Sinai. The midrash famously asks why God gave the Torah neither in the Egyptian diaspora, nor in the Land of Israel. Why was it given in the *midbar*, the wilderness? The answer is that the Torah

– or, if you will, Judaism – is not contingent on geography. It belongs to all Jews no matter where they may be. Since Mount Sinai we have all been very busy with the Torah, and done different things with it, no one expression better than the other. The test for authenticity and legitimacy is found in the ability of Jews in one context to give Judaism vibrancy while encouraging other Jews to do the same on terms of their own. All the while, in all its variations, we remember we are *am eḥad*, one people, in dialogue and partnership, equal and passionate stakeholders in a shared destiny.

Why Synagogue?

The most thought-provoking, most depressing – and for this room, most relevant – data to emerge from the recent studies of New York and American Jewry concerns the decline of synagogue life. According to the Pew study, 31 percent of Jewish respondents claimed to belong to a synagogue. Ten years ago, the percentage of Jewish households reporting synagogue membership was 46 percent. For those of us in the synagogue business, that is a precipitous and alarming drop. Most of us are well aware of the narrative taking place around the country: synagogues are contracting, often times merging, and in many cases collapsing. Here at Park Avenue our membership rolls are stable and growing, and in New York as a whole the numbers are above the national average: 44 percent of New York Jews claim to belong to a synagogue or congregation. But on the island of Manhattan, that number drops to a mere 32 percent. To put it another way: take away Borough Park, Williamsburg, the Five Towns, and Great Neck, and the pride and joy of North American Jewry should think twice before declaring itself ahead of the curve on at least one metric of Jewish vitality. Play with the numbers all you want, but the facts are the facts. Locally, regionally, nationally – synagogue life has taken a hit and is struggling desperately to regain its footing.

This morning, I want to think out loud with you on the following question: "Why synagogue?" There are more strategic plans, books, and blue ribbon studies out there than I can count. The commission called Synagogue 2000 was quickly replaced by another one called Synagogue 3000. People are asking all the right questions: How should dues be structured? What role can the national movements play in revitalizing local congregations? How should clergy be trained to lead congregations effectively? These are all good questions that need to be asked and – more importantly – answered and acted upon. But today I want to go to the very core of the matter: "Why synagogue?" Why, in a world of shifting Jewish demographics, limited philanthropic resources, and hyper-individualism, should synagogues exist at all? What precisely is the differentiated "value added" of a synagogue to American Jewish life? If we can't answer this fundamental question, then all the studies and strategic plans are but a rearranging of deck chairs on a sinking ship. We exist in a marketplace of ideas and unbridled choice. If adult education is what you want – you can take a class at Skirball. If social justice is your thing – American Jewish World Service (AJWS) and the American Jewish Joint Distribution Committee (JDC) do it better than we do. If you want to advocate for Israel – join AIPAC. If you want to hear a famous speaker – our budget cannot compete with that of the New York Historical Society. Want a personal relationship with a rabbi? By Monday lunch, I can get someone from Chabad to study with you. Beautiful music? Go to the opera or philharmonic. Need a social circle? There are golf clubs in Westchester dying for your membership. Tot services? Go to the 92nd Street Y for Shababa. And you know and I know that in this neighborhood, in this day and age, wanting your child to have a bar or bat mitzvah is not reason enough for a synagogue to exist. Rooms and rabbis can be rented easily enough. Gone are the days that you need to join a shul to celebrate bnei mitzvah. Synagogues are so big and clunky and cumbersome. Ours is an era of disintermediation. Whether we are shopping for groceries, books, or spirituality, if we can cut out the middleman, why wouldn't we? Why should the fate of synagogues be any different than that of Borders and Blockbuster Video? If we can't answer the question "Why synagogue?" then the honorable thing to do is to call it a day, pack up our things, and move on to the next big thing.

In order to give you an answer, or at least my answer, I need to take you a few steps back, actually a few thousand, specifically, to this week's Torah portion. Because it is here, during Israel's wilderness wanderings, that the very first Jewish communal structure was built. The *mishkan*, the mobile desert tabernacle, housed the ark of the covenant, the presence of God and the locus of Israel's ritual life. "Let them make for me a sanctuary," instructs God, "that I may dwell amongst them."

(Exodus 25:8) Israel's efforts and contributions are both individual and collective, and so too, the return on that investment. God's presence is felt among all the people and within each person, at each and every stage of the wilderness wanderings.

As we know from the haftarah reading usually associated with our parashah, as the Israelites gained a foothold in the land, as the Kingdom of Israel was established, King Solomon built his Temple. Modeled after the desert tabernacle, this shrine was also meant to house God's presence, to be an axis, if you will, connecting the heavens and the earth. No longer did the structure move with Israel, rather, the Israelites moved or made festive pilgrimages to the Temple on Pesah, Shavuot, and Sukkot. Offerings of thanksgiving, of guilt, of gratitude – the First and Second Temples addressed the full range of religious and communal experience. Note that the Hallel service which we say today in observance of Rosh Hodesh is the oldest of all our prayer services, dating back to the time of the Temple. A selection of biblical Psalms recited and sung with instrumentation – exaltations of God's bounty, petitions in times of peril, prayers of affirmation and thanksgiving. Compared to its initial setting – with thousands of pilgrims flocking to the Temple – today's Hallel is but a shadow of the Super Bowl halftime show that it must have been back then.

We know the Temple would be destroyed and the Israelites once again on the move, but – as today's actual haftarah from Isaiah makes clear – the desire to make God's presence manifest, to do so in the context of community, would remain. What the structure that accomplished that looked like and the manner in which it functioned would inevitably and necessarily reflect the context in which Jews lived. The more transient and mobile the community perceived itself to be, the more modest the structure – look at the classic prayer *shtiebel* of medieval *kehillot*. When a community of Jews established the first Reform temple in Hamburg in 1817, it was a statement not only of their claim to build a structure spiritually analogous to the Jerusalem Temple, but of their level of comfort in the German context. Just last month, members of our own community were in Newport, Rhode Island to celebrate the 250th anniversary of the Touro Synagogue, a powerful statement about the liberated and stable condition of Jews on American soil. As my colleague Dr. David Starr explains in his essay on the subject, the aesthetics of Jewish houses of worship (this one included) may be read psychologically – an "edifice complex," a window into the admixture of pride and anxiety Jews have wherever they may be.

This historical prologue would not be complete without at least mention of the most local and influential shaper of the conversation: Mordecai Kaplan. Next time you are on the West Side, take a look at The Jewish Center on 86th Street between Amsterdam and Columbus Avenues. In creating a ten-story structure whose mission extended well beyond a mere house of prayer – to include "a *shul* with a pool and a school" – Kaplan well understood the need for a synagogue to provide a sense of group identity, all the while enabling an acculturating American Jewry to be seamlessly integrated into civic life.

It is precisely this observation about Kaplan's vision that brings us back to the question with which we began. In this day and age, just shy of one hundred years since the founding of The Jewish Center, I no longer turn to the synagogue for my pool or gym – I turn to my own gym. If I want a social outlet – what some sociologists call a "third place" away from home or work – I go to Starbucks. Kaplan's vision for a synagogue as a communal meeting place worked in a time when Jews couldn't afford, had no access to, or weren't interested in what secular society offered – conditions that do not exist today. In fact, if Kaplan were alive today, he would demand that we once again reconstruct the central structure of Jewish life to fit the needs of American Jewry as it finds itself now, not one hundred years ago.

All of which means that the time has come to articulate with great clarity exactly what it is that a synagogue can provide that no other institution in the American Jewish landscape can. And the answer, the function of this synagogue – or any synagogue worthy of your attention – is not all that different from that which was stated in this week's parashah thousands of years ago: "That I may dwell amongst them." Only here, only in a synagogue, is the unique and infinite divinity of every human being brought into full relief in a communal context. One can go to the Grand Canyon to feel God's presence; one can, according to Jewish law, pray pretty much wherever one pleases. But only here, only in a synagogue, can you be part of a community whose operating assumption is that everyone – young and old, rich and poor, single and married, people you like and don't like – all of us exist equally, collectively, and covenantally in God's image and presence. With each birth, a new world begins that never existed before. With each death, we lose a life that can never be replaced. In sin, we arrive here knowing that despite our shortcomings, we may still seek spiritual rehabilitation and repair; our flaws do not preclude us from standing before God or our fellow humanity. Just the opposite, in this place we are reminded that God's presence dwells within sinner and saint alike. In our joy we come here to express our thanksgiving to God, singing Hallel today just as they did in the Temple of old. And in our sorrow, we come here to ponder the burdensome mystery of a world in which inexplicable pain exists. If God's presence is elusive, then a synagogue bears the promise that another person may brighten our darkness by way of the light of their divine spark, and together we may mend a broken world. And yes, here in this synagogue we read, commemorate, and ritualize the ongoing presence of God in the eternal narrative of our people – in the Torah, at the Exodus, at Mount Sinai, with the Jews of Shushan, and in the modern state of Israel. Every Shabbat, every new moon, every minyan, morning and night. The means are different and in constant need of reconstruction, but our mission – our *unique* mission – is remarkably akin to what it was from the beginning. To be a place where God's presence may be experienced, within each of us and among all of us, together as a community.

Finally, I would be remiss if I did not add one last dimension to the conversation. The differentiated mission of a synagogue is not just the presence of God, or to feel that presence in the context of a communal setting. The promise of a synagogue is that it is the only institution I can think of that seeks to sustain its mission over the course of a lifetime. High schools, colleges, and art museums are all important, but only a synagogue is there literally from cradle to grave. Think about the range of life in this building today, from newborns to senior citizens and everything in between. Here we see each other – ourselves and our children and grandchildren – go through life together. As a member of the clergy, this is without a doubt the most rewarding part of my job. Sanctity compounded over time – to be present at birth and bat mitzvah, wedding and birth again; in joy and in loss, in sacred relationship over time and, please God, a lifetime.

Religion was once defined for me as the project of building a world in which God would want to dwell. This Shabbat, let's hold off on the world, and focus on this place – our synagogue – demanding of ourselves and modeling for others what it takes to create such a place. The means will be different than in generations past. How could it be otherwise? The model has always evolved. But we have the brand, we have the mission, and it is as ongoing, unchanging, and compelling as when it was first articulated: "Build for me a sanctuary that I may dwell amongst them." We just need to be true to it, practice it, and let the divine light of this building radiate beyond our walls for others to follow.

It's Not About You

No matter how humble Moses may have been, I have to believe that the opening verses of this week's Torah reading hit him like a ton of bricks. "And you shall bring forward your brother Aaron, with his sons, from among the Israelites to serve Me as priests: Aaron, Nadav and Abihu, Eleazar and Itamar, the sons of Aaron." (Exodus 28:2) I wonder how Moses felt hearing from God that his brother would be put in charge of Israel's ritual life. Moses – who was plucked out of obscurity against his will, leaving a life of comfort, to lead a people not his own. Moses – who at great risk to himself went toe-to-toe with Pharoah, plague after plague. Moses – who courageously brought the Israelites through the sea to liberty and safety. Moses – who ascended Mount Sinai to receive the law, who time and again found the emotional wherewithal to forgive this mixed multitude for their murmurings and idolatry. Moses – who worked so hard to build the tabernacle according to precise specifications, a place where God's presence could dwell. And now, this week comes notice that someone else – Aaron – would be in charge. His brother and his brother's descendents would be the *Kohanim*, the priestly line. What I would give to know what Moses was thinking at that moment! A slap in the face. A bait and switch of, literally, divine proportions. To have worked so hard, to have given your all – your everything – for a cause, to have every reason to believe that you are "the guy," only to be told otherwise. The ball is in someone else's hands; you are not "the guy"; this story is not actually about you.

One of the finest studies by my teacher, Dr. Tikva Frymer-Kensky, *z"l*, was called "Moses and the Cults." It is a thought-provoking study of religious leadership, from the Hare Krishnas to the Moonies, from

Reverend Moon to Reverend Jim Jones. Her specific question of interest is the relationship between a leader and a cult, and the centripetal forces that often gather around charismatic personalities. Frymer-Kensky argues that despite the uprooted conditions and newly emancipated status of the Israelites, despite their obvious debt to Moses, despite all the reasons that might have led them to develop a cult around Moses, it never happened. Frymer-Kensky tracks a very subtle and moderating give and take on the matter of authority at each and every stage, the upshot of which is that the Israelites never succumb to the pitfall of deifying their leader – no matter how great Moses may have been.

Moses began as the sole and supreme magistrate of the people – a role that, a few weeks ago, was transformed, democratized, and, arguably, diminished, when at the urging of his father-in-law, Moses established a system of judges. Moses led the people militarily against Amalek, only to discover mid-battle that he needed the help of Aaron and Hur. This week, Moses is asked to cede ritual authority to his brother Aaron. Soon enough, political authority will be given over to his protégé Joshua. We know that ultimately Moses will not enter the land – a punishment not only for his having struck the rock, but for his overreaching claim that it was he, not God, who was responsible for drawing water from that rock. In prohibiting Moses from entering the land, God was not just delimiting geography, but signaling to Moses, to Israel, and to history that this journey was about something much bigger than Moses. Finally, of course, we are never told where Moses is buried; there is no pilgrimage site, no "dead hero cult" surrounding his personality. In summary, writes Frymer-Kensky, "Though remembered as a great man . . . he did not pass into folklore as a messiah."

Emerson's contention that every institution is the lengthened shadow of one man is not entirely true, not altogether responsible, and – it seems to me – not a terribly Jewish approach to leadership. Any institution – religious, political, or other – depends on strong leadership. We would not be here were it not for the Moseses, the Miriams, the Maccabees, and others of our people's history. But critical as great leaders may be, neither leaders nor, for that matter, the communities they lead should confuse a person with the principles that person is meant to serve. Moses had a specific role to play on behalf of his people and their cause, but he was not the cause itself. It is not without significance that Moses' name never appears in this week's parashah, an omission that is codified in the Passover Haggadah. To be free, to receive the Torah, to enter the land of Israel – these were the values for which Moses' leadership was necessary, values that were meant to extend well beyond his tenure. As the management guru Jim Collins explains in his study of the subject, the highest form of leadership is marked by "the paradoxical blend of personal humility and professional will." (*Good to Great*, p. 20ff.) Not only, argues Collins, are modesty and ambition not incompatible, but they are actually interdependent; the fierce resolve of effective leaders is contingent on their being self-effacing. Be it Abraham Lincoln, a corporate CEO, or the captain of a Little League team, a leader's ambition must be first and foremost for an institution and its principles, never for him- or herself. In fact, one could argue that it is in the cultivation of successors, in exercising the muscle of stewardship, that we prove ourselves to be most vested in our principles. Just this week, I had lunch with an elder statesman of our community who, before stepping down as chair of a major organization, understood it as his obligation to fill his board with individuals at least a generation his junior. If we really believe in the organizations we proclaim to lead, then it would follow that we create the mechanisms by which an organization's mission can extend beyond our tenure. If we fail in this regard, one could argue, we fail not just the test of ego, but we have failed the very ideals we claim to fight for so dearly.

But all of this doesn't make it any easier. Not for Moses, not for anyone with a type-A personality, is it easy to hear that "it's not about you." Each one of us is prone to believe that we are irreplaceable in our roles. Each one of us thinks that it is our unique imprint that is essential to an institution. It is not an either/or, and we all have to be very careful when threading this needle. And, of course, whenever we see leaders come and go, there will be anxiety as to whether or not the baton will be passed successfully. All of which means that no matter where we fall on the leadership matrix, both we and our institutions are better served by focusing not on people and nameplates, but on purpose and mission. I am often reminded of the first meeting between God and Moses, when Moses pleads to know God's name. God refuses Moses' request, sharing only *ehyeh asher ehyeh*, "I will be that which I will be." The midrash explains that God demurred because it was not the divine name that God wanted Moses to focus on, rather the divine attributes. God didn't need Moses to invoke his name; God wanted Moses to walk in His ways. That is what mattered most, that was what would bring honor to God.

The enduring image of this week's Torah reading is the investiture of the priests, the ornate garments that Aaron and the priestly line were instructed to wear. The sensitive reader of the Torah is already looking ahead to the not-too-distant future, when – in *parashat Hukkat* in the book of Numbers – it is time for Aaron to be gathered unto his kin. The two brothers Moses and Aaron ascend Mount Hor with Aaron's son Eleazar. With great care and compassion, Moses removes his brother's vestments one by one, and places them on his nephew, who, upon Aaron's death, assumes his father's leadership position. Emotional as the scene may be, the message is clear enough, to Aaron, to Moses, and most of all to Israel, then and now. Good leaders may be irreplaceable, but the great ones remember that the office they hold, the institutions they represent and the values they – and we – hold sacred, must transcend the limitations of any single person. It isn't easy, but this is the model to which we must aspire, for ourselves, for our community, and most importantly, for the ideas and ideals that are far greater than any one of us.

God Enough Sometimes Is

In a commencement speech to the 2005 graduating class of Kenyon College, the late David Foster Wallace began his remarks with the following parable:

Two young fish were swimming along and happened upon an older fish swimming in the opposite direction. The older fish nodded at them saying, "Morning boys, how's the water?" The two young fish swam on for a bit and then eventually, breaking the silence, one of them looked over at the other and said, "What the heck is water?"

The point of the fish story, for Wallace and for us today, is that it is inevitably the case "that the most obvious and most important realities are often the ones that are hardest to see and talk about." Today it is that kind of topic I want to discuss: God. Given Oscar season, I will begin with a spoiler alert: my sermon will conclude by affirming my belief in God. Given the size and diversity of this congregation, there is a statistical probability that not everyone in this room shares my belief. There may be one or two or ten or twenty members of this congregation who harbor doubts about what to me is as obvious as the water in which a fish swims. I can even imagine that here in this room are proud, card-carrying, dues-paying members of this community, who love Judaism, the Jewish people, and the state of Israel, who are fully invested in the successful transmission of Yiddishkeit from generation to generation, but who – when it comes to God – are the loyal opposition. "I get it," goes the argument, "there was a time and place when belief in God was a driver of personal and group identity, morality, and metaphysics. But that time and place are no longer, that belief is passé and anachronistic. To paraphrase the words of Rabbi Mordecai Kaplan: "Religion conceived in terms of supernatural origin is the astrology and alchemy stage of religion. [Ours] is the astronomy and chemistry stage of religion." (*Judaism as a Civilization*, p. 399)

The topic is a big one – there have been one or two books written on the subject – and our time is short. So this being New York, I want to approach it the only way that New Yorkers know how to discuss anything – quickly and self-referentially. I'll tell it by way of two rabbinical giants who were colleagues and friends. One, a predecessor of mine here at Park Avenue Synagogue, Rabbi Milton Steinberg, and the other – his teacher and mentor at the SAJ on 86th Street – Rabbi Mordecai Kaplan. If you are a regular, then you may have noticed an uptick in Kaplan references lately. He was the founder of Reconstructionist Judaism, and this spring marks the eightieth year since the publication of his monumental volume *Judaism as a Civilization*. My Tuesday evening class is studying his life and thought, and next week I will be presenting at a conference on him at Georgetown University. This morning, I want to focus on one particular aspect of his life – his relationship with Rabbi Steinberg, specifically, on the subject of God – a topic where, we shall see, Steinberg was Kaplan's most distinguished, devoted, and dissenting disciple.

Mordecai Kaplan had a very textured if not complicated relationship with God. At one and the same time, he "thought about God and the belief in God almost every day of his life," and yet was "the most famous naturalist the Jewish people has ever produced," (Mel Scult, *The Radical American Judaism of Mordecai M. Kaplan*, p. 133) For him as a rabbi, philosophy alone would not suffice; Kaplan may be best described as a religious humanist. His biographer Dr. Mel Scult relates a telling entry in Kaplan's diary on the day that four JTS rabbinical students paid him a visit, asking if they could serve the Jewish people with a non-theistic expression of Judaism. Kaplan wrote: "I told them plainly they could not do [so], since as rabbis their main function was to maintain the identity and continuity of the Jewish tradition. That tradition minus the God belief," Kaplan wrote, "is like the play of *Hamlet* without Hamlet." (Scult, p.145) Throughout his life – in his books, sermons, and diaries – God was a necessary and constant presence in Kaplan's writings.

And yet, in studying Kaplan, or any theologian for that matter, it all depends on what you mean by the word "God." "Words, like institutions, like life itself," wrote Kaplan, "are subject to the law of change." (*Judaism as a Civilization*, p. 398) One should not be misled into believing that by retaining the "God" vocabulary of the ancients, Kaplan meant what his predecessors meant. In other words, Kaplan did not subscribe to the notion of a supernatural providential deity." (Scult, p.132) He used words like "transnatural" and "supranatural" to describe God, but never "supernatural." Kaplan interpreted God as "the sum of the animating, organizing forces and relationships which are forever making a cosmos out of chaos." Or, as is often quoted, God is "the power that makes for salvation." To this day, I am not entirely sure what all this means. It doesn't make it easier that Kaplan wrote unsystematically, often inconsistently, and over a very, very long, long time; he lived to 102. But to return to our New York setting, remember that Kaplan's book was published in 1934, the same year as John Dewey's *Common Faith*. (As it happens, they both lived on West 115th Street.) Whether the influence was direct or simply in the air, both men readily assigned the word "God" to certain idealized qualities to which individuals or societies aspire – like justice, beauty, piety, and creativity. In Kaplan's mind, for Judaism to be viable, the God-Idea must be part of it, but in calling it the "God-Idea," and not "God," Kaplan showed his naturalist hand. Kaplan knowingly and consistently differentiated his theological stance from that of his Jewish predecessors. It would be a mistake to reduce Kaplan's God to simply the "good that we do," but all acknowledge the theological tightrope he walked between an immanent and transcendent God, a God who is merely a process, ethical ideal, or inner illumination, and a God who exists as a distinct entity beyond human consciousness.

All of which, in Rabbi Steinberg's estimation, fell short. The esteem in which Steinberg held Kaplan cannot be overstated. When I visited the Steinberg archives, I found ample record of the intellectual, professional, and personal debt Steinberg owed his teacher. They collaborated on building a movement, on publishing prayer books, on matters of the heart and of the mind. Notwithstanding this debt, or perhaps precisely because of it, Steinberg was also unflinching in critiquing his teacher. Steinberg didn't believe for a second that God was a long-beard who literally brought on plagues and split seas, but Kaplan's "God Idea" left Steinberg entirely wanting. In Kaplan's theology, wrote Steinberg, "Does God really exist or is he only man's notion?" In Kaplan's metaphysics, remarked Steinberg, "The universe is left unexplained. To say of God that He is a power with the scheme of things leaves the scheme altogether unaccounted for." (Rabbinical Assembly Address, 1949) And as Steinberg said from this very pulpit just months before he died, "To me it makes a great deal of difference whether God is an entity, a being in Himself or whether He is an aspect of reality." (Stenographed lecture notes, Steinberg Archive) Steinberg's tragic death at the age of 47 denied him the opportunity to express what his developed theology would look like. What is clear is that Steinberg understood faith as a different and complementary muscle group from philosophical reasoning. Steinberg knew Kaplan's love of Judaism and the Jewish people as well as anyone, but in failing to embrace a Supernatural God, a God with a consciousness and a will, Kaplan had jettisoned the very sacred vocation for which Judaism was intended in the first place. Such a Judaism would be akin to assembling the entire *mishkan*, the desert tabernacle in all its commanded and painstaking details, and then forgetting that the whole point was to house God's presence. In Steinberg's mind, Kaplan's God was "not God enough."

The God debate between Kaplan and Steinberg may appear – both in its moment and in retrospect – of little consequence, a modern-day "How many angels can dance on the head of a pin?" Their positions, we may say, differ only in degree, not in kind, neighboring shades on the theological spectrum. And while that might be true, that is also exactly the point. I would contend that it is precisely in this narrow space, or better yet, in the give-and-take between Kaplan and Steinberg that most of North American Jewry still exists. Long gone are the days that any Reform, Conservative, or even Orthodox Jew subscribes to a premodern or fundamentalist view of God. Very few Jewish clergy insist on a literal understanding of the text with talking snakes, a world in which evil comes as punishment for sin, and a God who elects one group of humanity over another. Kaplan, to put it squarely, had a point. But what Steinberg understood, and what we all know to be the case, is the power of standing before God in prayer, the drama of fulfilling a commandment in response to the divine will, and the urge to understand what it is that God wants of us. All of us search for meaning, each one of us longs for greater purpose, and each of us, I imagine, has at some point asked the question of how we fit into the grand narrative of existence. For me, belief in God – not the God Idea – but *God*, is not only satisfying, not only inspiring, but also, with all its problems, altogether reasonable. For many in this room my answer may not work; your response may be different than mine. The debate between Kaplan and Steinberg matters deeply because it covers territory that in many respects remains altogether resonant and relevant to this day.

Ultimately, the most important thing Kaplan and Steinberg shared was not their views, and not even, for that matter, their friendship. The most important thing they shared was a questing spirit – what Heschel would refer to as "radical amazement." A poetic if not romantic appreciation for the enigma of existence, the depth of the human soul, and the humble acknowledgement that there will always be far more about this world that we do not know than we do. Both men thirsted for God, both men sought to articulate answers of spiritual and intellectual integrity and intensity, and both men worked tirelessly on behalf of the Jewish people. Did they disagree? Of course they did – as can we. But we swim together as they did, side-by-side, seeking to understand, express, and respond to the most important mysteries of our lives.

On Religious Leadership

Goldstein was pulled over by the police one night around two in the morning. After checking over his ID and noting his advanced age, the policeman asked Goldstein exactly where he was headed at that time of night. Goldstein replied, "I am on my way to a lecture about the abuses of alcohol, its toxic impact on the human body, and the harmful side effects of smoking and late nights." The officer responded, "Really? And who exactly is giving that lecture at this time of night?" To which Goldstein replied, "Mrs. Goldstein."

Our world, broadly speaking, may be divided in two: the world as it is, and the world as it could or should be. Take any issue, whether it's global, like the environment, or personal, like how we treat our bodies. There is the descriptive, the state of affairs on the ground, and there is the prescriptive, the unrealized condition of how things "ought" to be. On one side is how Mr. Goldstein behaves, and on the other is how Mrs. Goldstein tells him he should behave. In philosophic terms it is what John Dewey identified as the gap between the real and the ideal. The most interesting element is not the recognition of the two worlds, and not even the awareness of the discrepancy between them – that who or where we are is not who and where we should be. The most interesting part is the interplay between the two – in other words, that Mr. Goldstein has chosen to come home at all! He knows what he is doing, he knows what his missus is going to say, he knows they are not one and the same thing, and yet embedded in him must be not only a moral compass to show him the way home, but a gravitational pull that brings him there every night even if he knows that upon walking in the door he will only be reminded of how he has fallen short. A combination of guilt and loyalty tugs at him, and maybe an unspoken hope that while he knows he falls short and may even continue to do so, he can always come home and one day perhaps that gap will narrow, and who he is and who he knows he can be will one day become one and the same.

Rabbi Abraham Joshua Heschel once wrote that "Faith is a blush in the presence of God." (*Man Is Not Alone*, p. 91). If I understand Heschel correctly, he is signaling that the purpose of this building, or any house of worship for that matter, is to alert us to the gap between who we are and who we know we can be, an awareness that induces us to blush. Like the *mishkan*, the desert tabernacle of this week's Torah reading, the goals of this house of God are both to draw you in and welcome you home, and paradoxically, to remind you of the work that still needs to be done – in this world and within ourselves. Lest we forget, the Hebrew word meaning "to pray" is a reflexive verb, *l'hitpallel*, literally "to judge oneself." Not to affirm who you are, but to remind you that there is often a gap between who you are and who you can be. Reminding you to mind the gap, mind you, is only the first goal. The second and far important role of this institution is to provide the path and the motivation by which that chasm can be bridged, so that we can mend ourselves and in doing so, let the radiance of this place mend this world in which we live.

All of this makes the job of a rabbi really, really, really interesting. Because if the project of religion is to inform, inspire, or admonish people towards bettering ourselves and the world in which we live, then it follows that my task must be the same. I am not here to describe the world as it is, or you as you are. For that you can read a newspaper or see a therapist. My job, no different than Mrs. Goldstein, is to tell you how you should be! Do you treat each other kindly? I don't know, but I know we should. Do you give charitably? Some of us may, some may not, but I am here to remind you of our obligation to do so. Are you faithful to your spouse? Statistically speaking, odds are that not everyone in this room is. But as a teacher of our tradition I can tell you unequivocally that we should be. Do you have kosher homes? I have no intention now or ever of checking cupboards, but . . . You get the idea. We live in an age of radical autonomy and permeable social boundaries. You know that I know that you know that at the end of the day your choices are – yours. Ever since the Enlightenment, rabbis have no longer possessed the political authority, inclination, and in my case, the time to check up on what Jews are and aren't doing. The only thing a rabbi or any religious leader can command in this day and age is respect. But just because the dynamics of the playing field have changed, doesn't mean the values have. I want you to be kind, I want you to be faithful to your spouse, I want you to be charitable, I want you to keep kashrut and Shabbat. As your rabbi, I want and expect you to do all sorts of things. I believe that the role of the rabbi is, as the saying goes, to comfort the afflicted and afflict the comfortable. And you know what I think? I think you want me to want you to do those things! You want me on that wall, you need me on that wall. You may or may not actually do these things, and in most cases only you and God will know. But even in modernity, especially in modernity, sound religious leadership demands not that I parrot the choices you would otherwise make, but rather that I inspire you to a life that you may not otherwise lead. The explicit or implicit social contract between the rabbi and the modern Jew is not to describe the world as it is, but the world as it could be. We enter this space precisely because it calls on us to reach beyond what everyone else, everywhere else, tells us is inevitable and unavoidable.

I think very carefully about what I do and don't state as values. You may agree with some and disagree with others. I believe that men and women stand equally before God, at the Torah and in prayer and everywhere. I believe that homosexual relationships should be sanctified no differently than heterosexual ones. I believe that to live in this moment of American Jewish history and not advocate on behalf of the miracle of the modern State of Israel is to abdicate your responsibility as a Jew. I believe that we should all be sending our kids to Jewish summer camp. And yes, as long as I am your rabbi, I will be preaching the paramount importance of endogamy – one Jew marrying another Jew. I preach these things because I believe them, because I believe they are justified by the tradition, and because I believe that each of these behaviors, among others, offers the greatest possibility for the growth, strengthening, and defense of the Jewish people. I am aware, well aware, that many in this community, many in this room have chosen and will continue to choose otherwise. But stating a Jewish value can never be contingent on the assent of the Jew in the pew. As a former member of

Congress recently reflected: "Real leadership is not about telling your opponents what they need but don't want to hear but telling your supporters." Or as Rabbi Israel Salanter stated: "A rabbi whose community does not disagree with him is no rabbi." Sitting in this room you should be challenged, you should be forced to revisit your assumptions; this space should, at one and the same time, embrace you like your home and prompt you to grow.

All said, however, the most critical element in any discussion on religious leadership has nothing to do with where you are, nor with the Jewish values preached from this pulpit. The most important thing you need to know is about me: that I struggle too. You need to know that long before I was a rabbi, I was just a Jew – just like you. I have no idea who my children will marry. I have no idea how long I can keep bringing my kids to shul and sending them to Jewish day school and Jewish summer camp before they hit system overload. I can't even claim to know for sure what combination of Jewish experiences holds the greatest promise for their Jewish future. I have stayed up more nights than I can count wondering if in this day and age if it is conscionable for me to live anywhere but the State of Israel. There are a lot of ideals that I believe should be held sacred, and I will be the first to admit that I myself don't live up to all of them. And while some may call that hypocrisy, the words I would choose are authenticity and integrity. The most honest and effective form of religious leadership I can provide for you is not to pontificate, but to share my struggles with you, to let you know even rabbis don't have it all figured out and so I don't expect you to have it figured out either. When I walk into this building, I am trying to traverse that gap between the person I am and the person I should or could be just like you are. That, incidentally, is what it means to be one of the Children of Israel. Not a promise to have it all figured out, but a commitment to wrestle with God's will – today, tomorrow, and every day of our lives.

One of the most moving passages offered by our tradition comes towards the end of the Torah when Moses enjoins his people to live a life of mitzvot: "It is not in the heavens . . . neither is it beyond the sea . . . no, it is very close to you, in your mouth and in your heart, to observe it." (Deuteronomy 30:12-13) Our faith, our tradition, our Torah, and our tomorrows are not meant to mirror our today. We do not live in the world as it ought to be and this place reminds of that fact. But this place also inspires us towards leading that life and it reminds us that it is not as distant as we think; the drive is not so far and the door is open if we are willing to enter it. It is altogether doable. Most of all, here in this space, we acknowledge and embrace that we are all engaged in this struggle together, every one of us reaching out even as we admit to being unsure of what it is we seek to grasp, all of us humbly seeking to know and make real God's will here on earth.

Sh'mini/Shabbat Parah
On Ritual Innovation

It was this Sabbath, *Shabbat Parah* of 1922, that American Jewish history and arguably all of Jewish history changed forever, and in my opinion, for the better. Less than a mile away from here – on 86th Street and Central Park West, at the Society for the Advancement of Judaism, twelve-year-old Judith Kaplan, the daughter of Rabbi Mordecai Kaplan, was called to the bimah for her bat mitzvah. She recited the *brakhah*, read a portion of the Torah in Hebrew and in English, and changed the course of our people forever. "No thunder sounded," Judith Kaplan later recalled, "no lightning struck . . . and the rest of the day was all rejoicing." Truth be told, the world did not change overnight. It was not until 1931 that the first girl was called up as a bat mitzvah in a Reform synagogue, and by 1948 only about one-third of Conservative congregations conducted bat mitzvah ceremonies. But here we are, just shy of one hundred years since that propitious date, and neither we nor the kosher catering industry could imagine Jewish life without bat mitzvahs. The ritual itself may not be uniform, but its practice has become axiomatic for Reform, Conservative, and even many Orthodox communities. Today the passage of Jewish girls into womanhood is marked no differently than that of Jewish boys into manhood – a momentous ritual innovation that continues to shape Jewish life and living.

Ritual innovation is never a simple process. Religious or secular, private or communal, we count on our rituals to be stable; they are the touchstones of our identity. We attend public events expecting them to begin with the singing of national anthems. At the seventh inning of a baseball game we instinctively stand up with tens of thousands of strangers to sing "Take Me Out to the Ball Game." On those rare occasions that the New York Jets do move the football ten yards forward, we know to say, "And that's a Jets . . . First Down!" Most rituals are far less public and conscious. Think of the "pleases" and "thank yous" and other social graces that pepper our days. Rituals are the stable and shared language by which bridges are established between individuals or among groups of people.

As Jews we know that this is only the tip of the iceberg. We may call ourselves the "People of the Book," but it is our rituals that define who we are as a people. It could be our rites of passage, from brissen to bat mitzvahs, to breaking glasses under the huppah, including the customs of the shiva house. It could be waving the *lulav* on Sukkot, spinning a dreidel on Hanukkah, or bringing in Shabbat by lighting the candles. Our rituals don't just connect us to each other, they prompt us to draw from our sacred past. Think about how many rituals are codified into the Passover seder that we will celebrate in a few weeks. The intended and cumulative effect is stated: To "see ourselves as if we came out of Egypt." Rituals operate in what ritual theorists call the subjunctive tense, a world of "as if," a world that although it is not our actual reality, defines our identity. (Seligman, et. al., *Ritual and Its Consequences*) Most of all, rituals give expression to a nonverbal world which would otherwise lack expression. Ask anyone who has had a piece of clothing torn upon the passing of a loved one, placed a shovelful of earth into an open grave, beaten their chest in true contrition over a wrong that cannot be righted, or watched their child stand at the Torah for the first time. Ritual done right accesses a place in the human soul that cannot be reached by words or by any other means. Ritual done right is not only critical to who we are as Jews, but sits at the heart of what it means to be human.

All of which is why, when we change ritual, or worse, bungle it or fumble it, people get very, very sensitive. As many here know, my parents are British. As many may not know, my dad doesn't like turkey – never has, never will. To this day, I recall with great horror the year that my English mother – as a gesture of love for my dad – prepared Cornish hens for Thanksgiving dinner. Intellectually, who cares? It was one bird switched out for another. Intellect, however, has nothing to do with it. For me and my American-bred brothers, the memory of that Thanksgiving dinner without turkey sits like an open wound. The danger of innovation is, I believe, the message of today's Torah reading. It is never stated what the sin of Aaron's two sons Nadav and Avihu actually was. And there is certainly never any indication that whatever their sin was, it merited the punishment it received. All the text says is that they offered an *eish zarah*, most often understood as an alien or foreign fire, but more simply translated as something "different." The prior verses provide specific instruction on how to make an offering but Nadav and Avihu (like my mother) did otherwise. Was it good? Was it bad? We don't know, and that's not the point. All we know is that it was different: different than instructed, different than expected, different than what came before. It was different. They innovated and they paid the price – a rather large one at that.

It is precisely because we take ritual so seriously, that whether it is Nadav and Avihu or Mordecai Kaplan, there is a natural inclination to resist and reject anything that is different than what came before. We know that every ritual, from the red heifer ritual of today's *maftir* to the bat mitzvah ceremony, was by definition initially an act of innovation. In the words of the University of Virginia's Dr. Vanessa Ochs, "Part of the efficacy of rituals is that we can easily trick ourselves into believing that our invented rituals were never new, re-embraced or remade. But the fact is that all of our rituals were at one point created. They were new and then, because they were embraced, they became real." (*Contact: Journal of the Steinhardt Foundation*, Winter 2010, p. 6)

I love it when I get anxiety-filled phone calls from new parents asking about the permissible window for their daughter's baby naming – as if their daughter's Jewish identity is somehow contingent on a ritual that was not in existence for the first few thousand years of our people's history. Legal battles are waged for the right to display a Hanukkah menorah in public space alongside Christmas decorations, as if the integrity of our people is somehow hanging on our ability to do something that nobody did until 50 years ago. Intellectually, it makes no sense. But when it comes to ritual, intellect has nothing to do with it. Jews, but really all people, believe their ritual life to be stable, sacred, and inviolable – even, and sometimes especially, when it comes to rituals that are unto themselves innovations.

If there was ever a place where we could track this conversation, it is right here in this room. Let's start with some fun ones. Did you know that up until the mid-1980s, top hats and tails were standard High Holiday garb for our now increasingly open-necked bimah? Cantor Lefkowitz once shared with me that Cantor Putterman, *z"l*, did not allow the final stanza of *Ein Keloheinu*, whether he objected to its theology or maybe just wanted to get to kiddush a little sooner we don't know. For that matter, in the days of Rabbi Nadich, *z"l*, and Cantor Putterman *z"l*, *Kaddish Shalem* the full *kaddish*, was never recited – the leadership believing it to be a break in the flow of the service. Until 1958, this congregation used the Reconstructionist siddur, a prayer book that was burned publicly in midtown Manhattan by the Agudath Harabonim in 1945, the same year we adopted it. In fact, long after Rabbi Steinberg's tenure, many in this congregation continued to recite an alternative *brakhah* when called to the Torah, rejecting language of chosenness (*asher bahar banu mikol ha-amim*) for the softer option of being brought closer to God's service (*asher keravtanu l'avodato*). We used to stand whenever we said the s*h'ma*, but we don't anymore. There was never *duchenen*, the recital of the priestly blessing by *kohanim*, until Rabbi Lincoln's tenure, and it was only under the influence of the former chancellor of the Seminary that our community instituted the full Torah reading instead of the congregation's long-standing practice of the triennial Torah reading. I can give you a million more examples – when we bow, how we pray, the melodies and prayer books we use. The present-day very eclectic ritual life of Park Avenue Synagogue is a reflection of our idiosyncratic congregational history. Rituals have been retained and rituals shed based on the sensibility, needs, and aspirations of our congregational family at any given moment.

That process, to be clear, continues today. It is because I believe in the centrality of ritual in Jewish life that we must be as thoughtful about ritual innovation as we have always been. I am eyes wide open to the fear of the "different." But as sure as I am that the changes made by my predecessors did not come without their share of growing pains, I am doubly sure that the present strength of our community is a reflection of the trust, care, and courage with which those changes were made. Any changes we will make to our Shabbat morning service – the timing, the Torah reading, the length, the music – will be implemented with the same concern for the Jewish future as has always guided our congregational efforts. The specifics will change – they always have –

but the overall goal remains as constant as ever: To create a service of the mind and heart, responsive to those sitting in the pews *and* accessible to those seeking a point of entry. Will it be easy? Of course not. Will we get it right from the get-go? I doubt it. But if we trust each other, if we are willing to share a spirit of experimentation, and if we are intellectually honest enough to admit that every single thing we do, by definition, was at one time itself an innovation, then maybe, just maybe, our community can live up to being the laboratory of Jewish life we aspire to be.

For me, the most significant aspect of Kaplan's introduction of a bat mitzvah ceremony is not what took place on that particular Shabbat morning, nor for that matter, the fact that today we look back and wonder how it could ever have been otherwise. The scene that resonates with me is one that took place the night before in the Kaplan home, as Rabbi Kaplan sat with his daughter reviewing her Torah reading and *brochos*. There was a heated conversation between Rabbi Kaplan's mother and his mother in-law, that Judith Kaplan would recall with great clarity years later. "Talk to your son," said Kaplan's mother-in law to his mother. Tell him not to do this thing." Rabbi Kaplan's mother responded to her *macheteneste*, "You know a son doesn't listen to his mother. You talk to your daughter. Tell her to tell him not to do this thing." Ultimately, we know, neither grandmother prevailed. The event went as planned and Jewish history was forever changed.

It is not hard, not hard at all, for me to imagine what Kaplan was thinking as his mother and mother-in-law carried on in the next room over how best to convince him not to do what he was planning on doing. I hear those voices today – literally and figuratively. I am strengthened by words Kaplan would provide later in his life for what he did, the four "reasons" he instituted the bat mitzvah ceremony. What were they? His four daughters: Judith, Hadassah, Naomi and Selma. (Scult, *Judaism Faces the Twentieth Century*, p. 301). In those days and our own, it is the very love we have for our Judaism that calls on us to create a Jewish expression that speaks to the future stakeholders of our people. As such we will innovate and we will retain, we will do whatever is necessary in order to arrive at that vibrant place where we will, God willing, look back and wonder aloud to each other how it could ever have been any different.

Aharei Mot/Shabbat HaGadol
Strangers in a Land Not Their Own

If the wicked child were sitting at the Global Planning Table of the Jewish People rather than at the seder table, the response he would receive would be of a decidedly different and far more embracing nature. "What does this service mean to you?" the hutzpah-filled child asks. "To you and not to him – thereby excluding himself from the community." He stands in breach of a fundamental principle of our people, so much so, the Haggadah famously explains, that he must be struck in the teeth. "You who have placed yourself outside the Jewish community: Had you been there at the Exodus, you would not have been redeemed."

Nowadays, the Jewish communal reaction to the second child would be radically different. Our first response would be to create a blue ribbon study on engaging the unaffiliated. We would create a trip specially designed for such young adults – a ten-day all-expense-paid trip to Israel with the hope that disengaged Jews would retrieve that *pintele yid* buried deep within. On college campuses, we would identify a funder to underwrite free Shabbat meals, so as to remove any actual or perceived barrier to entering Hillel. If that second child had a family of his or her own, another Jewish foundation would send free Jewish children's books every month with the hope that bedtime could become a moment of Jewish identity building. For young professionals, we would create alternative spring breaks to India, Costa Rica, or Nicaragua to backdoor Jewish identity and connection through acts of social justice. "*Tatale*, don't beat yourself up," we now say to that second child, "if you can't connect to the Jewish community, we will send someone to your office to teach, provide an outreach worker 'to meet you where you are,' and be sure to check out our free High Holiday services in a converted warehouse with an open bar." These days, not only do we not heap scorn upon the Jew who sits at the periphery, but just the opposite: we pour enormous amounts of affection, energy, and resources into that disengaged Jewish soul.

In the 1990s, Jack Wertheimer, Steven M. Cohen, and the late Charles S. Liebman wrote an award-winning essay called "How to Save American Jews." (*Commentary*, Jan. 1996). It was written in the wake of the 1990 National Jewish Population Study that famously reported, among other signs of erosion in the Jewish community, the sobering statistic of an intermarriage rate of over fifty percent. The authors went on to distinguish between the different segments of American Jewish life: the "actively engaged," the "moderately engaged," the "loosely engaged," and then of course, the "disengaged." And while we could quibble with their classification and the criteria by which a person qualifies for each category, the stir the article caused was due to its prescriptive recommendations. The authors argued that the Jewish future would be better served by focusing resources on the core of affiliated Jews and not on those Jews sitting at the margins of Jewish life. Given the limited nature of Jewish resources, why would we do anything but direct our efforts at those already predisposed to affiliation? Day schools, synagogues, Jewish camping – these are the "in-reach" efforts that will bring the greatest return on investment. Well intended as it may be, outreach to the unaffiliated is throwing good money after bad. Besides they argued, if we are really interested in saving American Jewry, is it not a bit misguided to appeal to the lowest common denominator? Not only, their reasoning goes, does such a stance neglect those seeking an "authentic" Jewish expression, but Jews on the periphery are actually more likely to respond to traditional modes of Jewish expression, and not some bland, soulless "Jewish lite," denuded of the very substance that makes Judaism worth fighting for in the first place.

Twenty years and a Pew study later, the debate rages on, both in principle and pragmatics. With limited resources, shall we focus on the core or on the margins of communal life? It is not just a theoretical question, but one that plays out in my rabbinate all the time. Let me give you a recent example. A few Sundays ago, I officiated at a baby naming for a beautiful little girl. Neither the child nor the parents were members of the synagogue, but the grandparents were. They called me on behalf of their child asking if I, as their rabbi, could be present for the naming. From there, I went to a board meeting for a campus Hillel at a university attended by a disproportionately large number of young people from this congregation. The question on the table was how congregational rabbis can collaborate with Hillel directors to integrate our kids into Jewish campus life and then, hopefully, back into congregations after graduation from college. One of the many ideas discussed was the possibility of my spending a Shabbat on that campus next fall, inviting our kids and their friends for Shabbat dinner with their rabbi – and in doing so – deliver them, as it were, into the hands of the campus rabbi. Later that evening, I met up with a group of about eighteen successful young professionals, all but one unaffiliated, many children of this congregation, who, to their great credit, took time out of their schedules to serve meals to the homeless at the Bowery Mission. We did a mitzvah, they connected with each other and – despite the fact that they do not enter the synagogue other than on the High Holidays – in some circuitous way they connected to their rabbi and, by extension, their Judaism.

A baby naming, a Hillel meeting, an evening serving meals to the homeless, each act, I hope you will agree, worthwhile if not noble. But the thought did occur to me that under a strict definition of resource allocation, my time that day was not spent serving the membership of this community. "Rabbi," I can imagine some board member saying: "You are paid to serve the 1500 family units of this congregation. That time you spent with the unaffiliated young professionals should have been spent doing visits to home-bound congregants. That baby naming you did . . . if that parent is old enough to draw a paycheck and father a child, he can darn well join a synagogue. And as for you taking a fall Shabbat to make a campus visit, let's be clear – you are paid to be on the bimah of this synagogue week-in and week-out. Rabbi, it's not that any of these activities are objectionable, but if you spend your time running after those Jews who are not here, then you risk making the Jews who are here feel they are being taken for granted and – even worse – neglected."

There is no one crisp answer to the question, but it is the question of our time, and I think it can and should be added to your seder table discussions two days from now. The Haggadah is a story about many things – national liberation from slavery to freedom, the fulfillment of a divine promise, the recitation of sacred history. But at its core, I believe, the seder is about a journey – not only geographical, but also spiritual – a story of homecoming. "In every generation, you must see yourself as if you personally came out of Egypt." This is the objective, to feel yourself at home in the narrative of our people. It is a goal that remains elusive for far too many. Think about it. Why is the very first statement of the Haggadah not about welcoming those present, but acknowledging those who are not: "Let all who are needy come and celebrate Passover." Why does the entire ritual begin (*Mah Nishtanah*) and end (Who knows one?) with questions that immediately level the playing field? If there was ever a ritual attuned to the person coming in from the outside, it is the seder. It isn't just the wicked child who is alienated: three out of the four children have no idea what is going on. "From the beginning," the Haggadah clarifies, "our ancestors were idol worshippers . . . but now, we are called to God's service." The Haggadah's curricular goal is twofold. First, to encourage participants to identify with the core narrative of our people, and also to remind us of those who remain spiritually alienated, a demographic from which we can never disconnect because it is a demographic that once was us. As God said to Abraham: "Know well that your descendants will be strangers in a land not their own . . ." Even as, especially as, we gather at the seder table, we are made aware of those who remain in a condition of spiritual exile, and the Haggadah reminds us of our obligations to bring them back home.

Put simply, maybe the message of the Haggadah is that we, as a people, are a mixed multitude. From the four different kinds of children to the variations among contemporary Jews, we are not and have never been homogeneous. We need to be brought home by means as diverse as our varied constitutions. On a communal level, we must be willing to educate each other regarding the tipping points of Jewish identity and to be in constant dialogue on the roles that Jewish institutions play in impacting Jewish life. Day schools *and* Birthright, Jewish camping *and* campus outreach, AIPAC *and* AJWS. Yes, there are limited resources, but it is not an either/or proposition. As a synagogue, our first mission must be to articulate the unique role congregations like ours play as drivers of Jewish identity. In prayer, in study, in joy and sorrow, in community with each other and the greater people of Israel over a lifetime – no other institution can lay claim to our differentiated role. Yes, we are a membership organization – that is and will always be our first priority. But our mission extends beyond our walls and membership to young professionals, prospective converts, teens, and social justice projects, to name but a few. When it comes to Jewish identity, return on investment should never be measured strictly by way of members served. It is not an easy balancing act, and it is a struggle I face every day. In a sense, the task of a contemporary rabbi is no different than the role of the prophet Elijah as described in today's haftarah. "To turn the hearts of parents to their children, and those of the children to their parents." Religious leadership then, and now, is an act of mediating between the generations, helping each side understand, appreciate, and validate narratives and needs different from their own.

A final word: As I clicked to print this sermon yesterday, an email arrived in my inbox, at 3:13 pm to be exact. The sender was not a member in their own right, but a child and grandchild of congregants. I officiated at the wedding a few years ago, and knowing me, I imagine the question occurred to me in our pre-wedding meetings and at the Saturday night ceremony, how it could be possible that this bride and groom, both accomplished beyond their young years, just couldn't get around to sending in a shul membership form. I never said anything, we celebrated their wedding, and I never really heard from them again. So you can imagine my smile when I read the following words yesterday: "Dear Rabbi Cosgrove, We just wanted to reach out because although we already feel like we belong in the PAS community, we are interested in becoming official members of the synagogue and, in particular, getting involved in the young couple activities. How should we go about this? Thanks. Happy Pesach! Sent from my iPhone."

Nobody, not even a rabbi, can predict the timing or path of a person's return. But Passover teaches that if we leave our doors open, we never know who might just walk in. There are, in every generation, those longing to return, some who realize it, and others who don't. The story of redemption is ongoing. May the doors of our community, our shul, and our homes be wide enough to provide a homecoming to all who seek entry.

K'doshim/Rosh Ḥodesh Iyyar
Israel: Can't We All Just Get Along?

O f the towering figures of twentieth-century Jewry, few stood as tall as Rabbi Dr. Louis Finkelstein, z"l. A professor of Talmud and scholar of Jewish law, Finkelstein was appointed Chancellor of the Jewish Theological Seminary in 1940, a position he held with distinction until retiring in 1972. Finkelstein established the central role of the Seminary – if not of all of Conservative Judaism – in America. His leadership on interfaith affairs and his famed "Eternal Light" radio program, putting the voice of Judaism in the public square, provided Jews and Judaism a stature in the American landscape never experienced before. He offered the invocation at Eisenhower's second inauguration; he appeared on the cover of *Time* magazine. For a window of time, Finkelstein was the face and spokesman for American Jewry, to the degree that such a thing exists.

On the subject of Zionism, however, Finkelstein had a complicated relationship. As the scholar Naomi Cohen explains, although Finkelstein was a card-carrying member of the Zionist Organization of America, he opposed political and secular nationalism. In other words, while Finkelstein supported Palestine as a spiritual homeland for Judaism and the Jewish people, he saw no need for an actual state. Having grown up during World War I, Cohen explains, Finkelstein was part of a generation that "repudiated the militarism and hyper-nationalism that . . . had precipitated the world conflict." In Finkelstein's own words, "The primary question is not one of political control of the land . . . but whether the Jews are given the opportunity . . . to develop their spiritual and cultural life in the Holy Land." (private letter to Rabbi Milton Steinberg, cited in Naomi Cohen, "The Seminary and Zionism, 1902-1948") So adamant was Finkelstein's position, the story goes, that at one pre-state JTS graduation, the students' request to sing *Hatikvah* at commencement was turned down. In a charming act of defiance "the students arranged with the carillonneur at Union Theological Seminary (across the street) to play the melody . . ." in the midst of the proceedings.

One can only imagine what it was like in the 1940s – with the horrors of the Shoah, the refugee crisis, the strivings of Ben Gurion and the Yishuv, the pre-state Jewish community in Palestine – for an institution and leader of such stature to express such lukewarm support for the idea of a state of Israel. Great leaders such as Abba Hillel Silver of Cleveland, Solomon Goldman of Chicago, and one of my predecessors, Milton Steinberg of New York, had what to say. Did Finkelstein really envision Palestine, Steinberg asked, solely "as a community of saints . . .?" In a private letter to Goldman, Steinberg wrote, "I want Dr. Finkelstein . . . to stop pussyfooting on Zionism." A revolt of prominent rabbis led by Steinberg and Goldman emerged, a list of complaints was submitted, and demands were made that Finkelstein change his tune. In a sign of protest, Park Avenue Synagogue cancelled its annual fundraising appeal on behalf of JTS – Seminary Shabbat – a genuine intra-Jewish shoving match on the question of American support of Israel. (Naomi Cohen, "The Seminary and Zionism," in Wertheimer, *Tradition Renewed*.)

Today we announce the month of Iyyar, and with it the festival of *Yom HaAtzma'ut*, Israel's Independence Day. It is nearly seventy years since independence and I cannot help but wonder what, if anything, we have learned from our past. The issue of statehood, of course, became a moot point for American Jewry in 1948. The non-Zionist or anti-Zionist Jewish community both on the left and on the Haredi right have thankfully been marginalized to the sidelines. But while the personalities and politics have changed, the proclivity of American Jews to disagree among themselves over Israel appears to be as strong if not stronger than ever.

Let's begin with my inbox this week. With the Celebrate Israel Parade coming up on June 1, the emails are flying fast as to who can and can't march. A series of critics, ranging from local rabbis, known organizations like the ZOA, and individuals with an email account and too much time on their hands, have sown dissent in the community falsely claiming that left-leaning organizations like the New Israel Fund are advocates of Boycotts and Divestments against Israel. Such organizations, these people claim, are anti-Israel, anti-Jewish, and have no place marching in the parade. And while the mudslinging surrounding the parade may seem beneath the dignity of this room, it is, I believe, a data point of a bigger trend emerging on just how big the pro-Israel tent is in America these days.

Over the next few weeks, the Conference of Presidents of Major Jewish Organizations will consider the membership application of the politically left J Street. As with the parade, I am not entirely sure how many people care whether this conference – whose members include the Jewish fraternity AEπ – admits J Street, but the very possibility has raised the hackles of establishment figures in the Conference and beyond. Is there a place in the Conference for an Israel-loving organization that is willing to advocate policies in America contrary to those of the Israeli government?

Alternatively, turn your attention to college campuses. An entire movement has sprung up this academic year called Open Hillel. Should a Hillel, the question goes, give a platform to everyone, including those who express anti-Israel views? On the one hand, it is a matter of free speech and inclusivity: a campus of all places should allow for the free exchange of ideas. On the other hand . . . am I really writing a check to support a campus Hillel that offers programming that is not in lock-step with the Israeli government?

Two final examples, local ones that came and went. Just a few months ago, a student group at Ramaz, the local Orthodox high school, invited Rashid Khalidi, a Columbia scholar of the Middle East and voice for the Palestinians, to speak to the student body. The school administration rescinded the invitation the students had issued. The students responded by gathering a petition objecting to the administration's decision. Soon thereafter, The Jewish Museum similarly had to rescind an invitation it had made to the literary theorist

Judith Butler, who was to speak on Kafka. Why? Because Butler has voiced strong criticism of Israel and why would a museum for the Jews, funded by Jews, representing the Jews, provide space for such views?

The list goes on and on, and it is important to point out that not all these examples are the same. What goes on a college campus is different from a high school. There is a big difference between admitting J Street to the Conference of Presidents and allowing a supporter of BDS to speak at The Jewish Museum. But what the data points do collectively indicate is the emergence of a distressing moment for American Jewry. A polarizing and accusatory climate that is not only sad and unproductive but corrosive and dangerous for American Jewry, for the State of Israel, and for the all-important relationship between the two. Somewhere along the way we have lost the ability to house internal dissent. Technology provides the tools to turn every teapot into a tempest and we never seem to fail to create the opportunity to do so. There is nothing new about internal Jewish dissent. When it comes to Israel, the Steinberg-Finkelstein debate is but one of many examples when American Jewry disagreed on Israel. There are literally books and books written on the subject, and in many cases, the debates of yesteryear were far more critical to Israel's survival than some of the nonsense going on today. Maybe it is because of the clutter of the Internet age, maybe it is a byproduct of an American Jewry that has never been – at one and the same time – as strong and as assimilated as we are now and thus able and inclined to speak out against each other in public. I don't know. I just know that we have woken up to a "gotcha" culture of "who's-in and who's-out," with everyone looking over each other's shoulders: a pro-Israel neo-McCarthyism. Somewhere along the way we have lost the way. We have lost sight of the greater good. We have forgotten that more important than those things we disagree on are those things upon which we do agree.

Generally speaking, I avoid signing my name to communal letters. There are too many politics involved and I have seen far too many colleagues do so and get burned – misled and misrepresented – and then come to regret it. But it was with great pride that I recently added my name to the Jewish Community Relations Council statement regarding Israel dialogue. Among other things, the letter was a commitment by all who signed it to see our fellow members of the Jewish community as part of *klal yisrael*, the family of Israel. The commitment to treat others with decency and honor . . . to cherish what we have in common, even if we disagree with each other. The commitment to the Jewish teaching *derekh eretz kadma laTorah*, proper conduct precedes the Torah. Respectful speaking and listening are possible even in the midst of a heated interchange of ideas. (www.theisraeltalks.org/)

Proud as I am of being part of this cross-communal statement, my hope is that its sentiment infuses the spirit not just of our synagogue, but of the Jewish community as a whole. Israel is as prickly a subject as we have. How do we balance her very real existential threats with the condition of the stateless Palestinian living in Bethlehem? How do we reconcile the policies of the Israeli government with the fact that it is not at all clear to me how one makes peace with a people who don't recognize your right to exist? How do we, as a liberal Jewish community, turn to Israel as a source of strength and identity formation, when that very state does not recognize the form of Judaism practiced here in this building? There is no shortage of conundrums that Israel provides for me and for all of us. But there is a way to have the conversation – here in this building and beyond. There is a way to allow for free speech and yet recognize the difference between constructive and destructive debate. There is a way to fulfill the mitzvot in our parashah of reproving your kinsman and loving your neighbor as yourself at one and the same time. There is a way for our voice to be heard in Israel that positions world Jewry as caring and passionate and sometimes dissenting stakeholders in the Jewish state. There is a way to have robust dialogue, all the while being careful not to fuel the arguments of those who don't love Israel as much as we do. It will never be perfect, and it does mean we have to be a bit more circumspect when talking about Israel than about our favorite sports team. But if we can agree that greater than any of our disagreements is our love for each other and love for Israel, if we can fight for Jewish unity harder than we fight with each other, then the greater good, the good of Jewish unity, will always win out. It is not easy to take a position that dignifies a diversity of opinion, even those that are different from our own. But make no mistake, our synagogue has and will continue to model how such a conversation can be had. And yes, I expect to see you all marching on Fifth Avenue with me on June 1.

On May 6, Park Avenue Synagogue will welcome Professor Yehudah Mirsky to speak about the religious legacy of the late Rabbi Abraham Isaac Kook, the chief rabbi of pre-state Palestine. Rav Kook was a deeply pious man, but equal to his passionate faith was his love of Jews, no matter what their stripe, so long as they were engaged in building up the nascent state of Israel. Apropos of this season, Mirsky describes the events surrounding Passover of 1925. On the eve of Passover, Rav Kook and his students traveled to a militantly secular kibbutz near Jerusalem to offer them *matzot*, presumably to bring *Yiddishkeit* a little closer to this non-practicing community. Not surprisingly, the rabbi and his students were chased away by the non-religious pioneers. What was surprising was that two days later, on the first day of Passover, "Kook was attacked by young ultra-Orthodox zealots on his way to prayers at the Wailing Wall." In his attackers' eyes, a rabbi who would consort with secularists was nothing more "than a delirious supporter of the Left, and the Left of him." (Mirsky, *Rav Kook*, p. 192)

It is not easy, then or now, to take a position that understands the diversity of voices at the Jewish table as part of the greater good. It means there will be potshots taken from the left and from the right. It means that sometimes a win is not so much advancing your position, but advancing the unity of the Jewish people. It is a strange thing to fight for, but our world is in desperate need of people, of synagogues, and of communities willing to proudly assert such a stance. May each one of us, this institution, and the entire community fight hard to establish, sustain and defend this communal norm.

How Jewish Should the Jewish State Be?

In the pantheon of great rabbinic debates, the controversy between the Ridbaz and Rav Kook on the issue of the *heter mechirah* may not rank in the top ten or even twenty. The year was 1910, and the players were the Ridbaz, the Lithuanian scholar Rabbi Ya'akov David Wilovsky, and Rabbi Avraham Isaac Kook, the man who would go on to become the first Ashkenazic Chief Rabbi of pre-State Palestine. At the time, Wilovsky, an immigrant to Israel from Chicago, served as head of a Yeshiva in the northern town of Tz'fat, and Kook as the Chief Rabbi of the coastal city of Jaffa.

The background to their debate was rooted in this week's Torah reading. "Six years you may sow your field and six years you may prune your vineyard and gather in the yield. But in the seventh year the land shall have a Sabbath of complete rest, a Sabbath of the Lord: you shall not sow your field or prune your vineyard. (Leviticus 25:3-4) These are the laws of the sabbatical year, *shmittah*, a required rest for the land in ancient Israel's agrarian society. The laws serve as a reminder that the land belongs not to humanity but to God, that we must extend the earth an opportunity to lie fallow, and that the ancient farmer be afforded the chance to set aside economic competition in order to focus on those things in life that truly matter.

Compelling and poetic as the sabbatical laws may be, there is one very important caveat. For nearly two thousand years, while the Jewish people were exiled throughout the Diaspora, the *shmittah* laws were entirely theoretical – totally abstract in nature. There was no Jewish settlement in Palestine to speak of, no Jewish land to let lie fallow.

Until . . . one day . . . there was. With the first and then second waves of *aliyah* (immigration), at the turn of the twentieth century, Jews began to return to Palestine to establish the Yishuv, the pre-state community. When the *shmittah* year of 1910 approached, it was the first time, in a very, very long time that Jewish farmers asked themselves whether the laws of *shmittah* were to be kept. On the one hand, what is the promise of settling in our people's homeland if not an opportunity to observe the laws of our people as instituted by our Torah? On the other hand, the economic consequences of actually observing such a sabbatical year could be devastating to an already struggling and vulnerable community, potentially spelling disaster and collapse of the entire Yishuv.

To make a long story short, Rav Kook penned a 120-page treatise in which he deployed the legal fiction of a *heter mechirah*, a permissible and temporary sale of the land to non-Jews thereby enabling the land to be worked. No different than Jews selling *hametz* on Passover and other convenient loopholes of Jewish law, Kook's solution provided an elegant way out of the conundrum. If the land were no longer "owned" by a Jew, the obligations of *shmittah* no longer applied. In Rav Kook's opinion, not only was such a "sale" possible and permissible, but if it served to save the fledgling community from financial ruin, it was necessary.

As for the Ridbaz, he believed otherwise. Not only did he disagree with Rav Kook's legal reasoning, but he posited that Kook's proposed solution undermined the very goals it was designed to support. If it is sold, even as a legal fiction, the land is no longer Jewish and is thus deprived of its unique status and sanctity. Why settle the land at all, if we aren't going to embrace the totality of Torah law? That is the whole point. In the years to come, the Ridbaz, along with a number of other rabbis, denounced Kook for his lenient position that appeared willing to forgo the Jewishness of the land for another competing value. Ultimately, Rav Kook won the day. From 1910 right up to sabbatical year arriving this fall, the legal fiction of selling the land has been deployed every seven years, a concession made in order that the land of the Jewish people be made more livable for the Jewish people. (Morrison, *Sap-*

phire From the Land of Israel: A New Light on the Weekly Torah Portion, from the Writings of Rabbi Abraham Isaac HaKohen Kook)

Remote and picayune as the debate between Rav Kook and the Ridbaz may seem, at its core lies the issue upon which Israel continues to squirm right up to this day, namely: Just how Jewish should the Jewish State be? I know, at first blush, it seems like an awkward and even unseemly question to utter aloud. The whole point of Israel is to be a Jewish state. For two thousand years we longed for, prayed for, and died for our people's right to self determination. *Lihiyot am ḥofshi b'artzeinu*, to be a free people in our land. What do you mean? How can the Jewish state possibly be too Jewish?

The most important thing for Americans to understand about Israel is that the Israel is not America. Americans take the separation of Church and State as an article of faith. The first amendment's establishment clause was, in the words of Thomas Jefferson, "a wall of separation" between religious institutions and the federal government. It is by no means airtight. We need not look far to see misplaced Christmas wreaths, school prayers, and invocations of faith in the public square, to know that America is not entirely neutral when it comes to religion. But for the most part, or at least in principle, the democratic polity of America professes no religion of its own.

Israel's model is entirely different. Somewhat like other nations, Israel possesses an established church – a Jewish one. From the very get-go, the symbols, institutions, and laws of Israel have been Jewish. The national anthem *Hatikvah*, the public holidays, the menorah as a state symbol, the chief rabbinate – Israel is defined as a Jewish state. But while Israel is Jewish state, it is not a theocracy. Unlike Iran, Israel lays claim to being a democracy, a state governed by elected officials. In its founding declaration and subsequent Basic Laws, Israel promises "to uphold the full social and political equality of all its citizens, without distinction of race, creed, or sex." Yes, Israel is Jewish, but Israel also stands committed to liberal, democratic, and secular values.

It is a balancing act that makes life in Israel very, very interesting. To be a Jewish and democratic state is much easier said than done. Because whether it is the laws of the *shmittah* year, the days on which the buses run, or the rights accorded to non-Jews living in the Jewish state, Israel cannot escape the foundational Kulturkampf embedded in its

DNA. The question of just how Jewish the Jewish state should be continues to shape the national debate. Just this week, the Prime Minister of Israel threw his support behind a Basic Law that would affirm Israel as a Jewish state. Such legislation, while protecting the cultural, civil, and religious status of non-Jews in Israel, does not acknowledge their national aspirations. While the bill itself does not sound particularly revolutionary, it is understood both by its supporters and detractors as an attempt to tip the scales towards a heightened recognition of Israel's Jewishness to both Israelis and the outside world. Not surprisingly, Justice Minister Tzipi Livni declared her opposition to the legislation, refusing to allow "the damaging, weakening, or subjugating of [Israel's] democratic values to its Jewish values." The players and politics are different, but the debate is basically one and the same. Over one hundred years since the Ridbaz and Rav Kook, we are still arguing over just how Jewish the Jewish state should be.

And as with all great debates, our highest hope may be that the debate continues. The more I think about it, the more I think how disastrous it would be if either side were able to declare victory. The whole point of Zionism is to create a home for the Jewish people in the land of Israel. Now and forever, the Jewishness of the state of Israel must be affirmed and defended. Attempts to create some sort of bi-national state stripping Israel of its Jewish character would be a betrayal of thousands of years of Jewish longing. And yet those who love Israel – who truly love Israel – must also be the most vigorous defenders of the progressive instincts expressed in Israel's founding documents. No more problematic than a bi-national state would be a state that became so Jewish that it lost its ability to house the freedoms and rights of liberal democracy. There is a point when the Jewish state could become "so Jewish" that it loses its ability to be livable, and we must protect Israel from ever nearing that line. It is not a comfortable or clear state of affairs; it never has been. Like any uncomfortable marriage of principles, the scholar Steven Mazie explains, the Jewish and democratic nature of Israel is a status quo agreement "under which neither side is especially happy and each constantly attempts to gain a bit of ground on the other." (*Israel's Higher Law*, p. 32) It is a somewhat strange thing to fight for – to be uncomfortable – but we who care about Israel as much as we do need to make sure that the debate is nurtured, nudged, and celebrated into the future.

Perhaps most importantly, we must remember that the existence of this debate, while critical to Israel's soul, must always be conducted with great respect for the opposing side. As Yehuda Mirsky explains in his new book on Rav Kook, well after the *shmittah* year of 1910, the debate between the Ridbaz and Rav Kook continued – both publicly and privately. But while they disagreed, often vehemently, it was understood that their debate served a greater good – an exchange by which the name of God and the land of Israel would be strengthened and made sacred. In fact, so devastated was Rav Kook at the passing of the Ridbaz that he wrote to an associate that his "grief at [the] great loss at the departure of that *tzaddik* [righteous person] . . . makes it hard for [him] to think with peace of mind." (Mirsky, *Rav Kook*, p. 76)

So too in our own day. Yes, we must fight for Israel as a Jewish state. We must also fight for Israel as a democratic one. Most of all we must fight for an Israel that can be both Jewish and democratic at one and the same time. And no matter on what side of the debate we find ourselves, we must carry ourselves with great respect for those with whom we differ, acknowledging their wisdom even as we disagree, knowing all the while that the debate itself serves to strengthen a greater good which we all share in common.

B'ḥukkotai

Doing Jewish With Other Jews

One of the most intriguing, intelligent, and important articles written this year on the subject of Jewish identity came from a totally unanticipated and, at least to me, unknown source. The piece is called "The Rise of Social Orthodoxy: A Personal Account"; it appeared in last month's issue of *Commentary*. The author is Jay Lefkowitz, a New York lawyer who once served as the President's special envoy for human rights in North Korea. Though he is much published, scanning Lefkowitz's CV indicates that matters of Jewish identity are not his primary focus of concern – making his public reflections on personal religious practice all the more interesting.

At first glance, Lefkowitz's article reads like yet another self-congratulatory article written by an Orthodox Jew in the wake of the Pew study of American Jewry. With intermarriage and assimilation on the uptick and Jewish identity on the wane, the only pocket of good news is coming from the Orthodox. Unlike Conservative, Reform, or unaffiliated Jews, the intermarriage rates for Orthodox Jews remain low, the birth rates high, and the sense of Jewish identity strong. Ever since the Pew study was published, scores of such triumphantly-minded articles have been penned, schadenfreude-filled pieces picking apart the liberal arms of American Jewry, more often than not, from the cheap seats of Israel or, as I initially assumed with this article, the bosom of the Orthodox world.

As Lefkowitz's article progresses, what becomes clear is that the direction of his argument is actually far more interesting than the pot-shots of his Orthodox co-denominationalists. With refreshing candor, Lefkowitz shares that the "secret sauce" of the Modern Orthodox community is not its ideology. Because unlike the intellectually closed Haredi community on the far right, Modern Orthodox Jews are fully immersed in the debates of our time: women's rights, gay rights, ordaining female clergy, shared participation in prayer services, to name a few. You may have read recently of mainstream Orthodox schools in New York permitting women to wear tefillin. Lefkowitz shares the open secret of Orthodox teens texting and using technology on Shabbat, eating vegetarian in non-kosher restaurants and engaging in all sorts of other "un-Orthodox" practices.

Lefkowitz's laundry list of "foot-faults" in the Orthodox community reminds me of the story related to me by the owner of a Manhattan Kosher Deli who was approached some years ago by a local Orthodox rabbi. Though the deli was kosher, it was open on the Sabbath, and because of that, it lacked certification as kosher by the Orthodox rabbinate. Believing he could play to the owner's business instincts, the rabbi pleaded, "If only you closed on Shabbat, then I could stand before my community and announce the news that you are kosher and all my congregants could then eat in your restaurant!" To which, the deli owner matter-of-factly replied, "Rabbi, all your congregants already eat in my restaurant."

But even more interesting in my mind than the private practices enumerated by Lefkowitz are the theological ones. Namely, that because Modern Orthodox Jews are both modern and Orthodox, literalist readings of the Torah are passé. The Torah may or may not be the revealed word of God. The world is not five thousand plus years old, evolution is taught unapologetically in school. The theology or ideology of these Orthodox Jews is not, it would seem, quite as Orthodox as we would otherwise believe.

All of which leads us to the point of the article. If Modern Orthodox Jews are neither intellectually nor socially segregated from the world at large; if they look, believe, and sound, in some sense, like Conservative Jews of a generation ago – then what exactly is the key to their demographic strength? The answer, in a word, is community. Lefkowitz explains that Orthodoxy is strong and growing because

Modern Orthodox Jews have committed to living "intensive Jewish lives." They may not be Orthodox in practice or theology, but they are, as the title of the article indicates, "socially Orthodox." The language, the literature, the calendar, the institutions, the land, the Sabbath, and yes, the rituals of the Jewish people serve as the foundation for a robust and resilient Jewish identity. The communal assumptions of Modern Orthodox Jews – where one lives, vacations, spends time, spends money – all point to what sociologists call "a thick sense of Jewish identity." The observances of Modern Orthodox Jews are determinative not owing to their belief in being literally commanded by God, but rather because their practiced Jewish behaviors cultivate a sense of Jewish belonging. The connective tissue they form, at Shabbos tables, shivah houses, gap years in Israel, and holiday cycles collectively contribute to a self-imposed kinship with other Jews. They are socially Orthodox, and it is a communal posture that has made all the difference.

All of which got me thinking. If the upshot of Lefkowitz's article is that the key to Jewish identity and continuity is not what you believe, but what you do and with whom you do it, then the implications extend well beyond the relative merits of Reform, Conservative, and Orthodox Judaism. If Lefkowitz is right, then ideology is entirely secondary to sociology, or to put it more simply, what matters most is whether you "do Jewish with other Jews." Yes, Orthodoxy has a competitive advantage in that it has a built-in system of observance by which to generate a sense communal belonging – but it is not the only way. Identity formation and group affiliation is not the provenance of any single denomination of Jewish life. Ask any person who went to Jewish summer camp – Reform, Conservative, or Orthodox. What made it work? Doing Jewish with other Jews. What about Birthright? It has no ideology, but it has transformed Jewish life. Why? Again, doing Jewish with other Jews. What about the State of Israel? Doing Jewish with other Jews – on a national scale. We can go down the list – synagogues, youth groups, day schools, year-abroad programs, any program able to generate and sustain a deep sense of communal connection – these are the institutions and efforts that produce a thick sense of Jewish identity for the contemporary Jew.

Ever since the Enlightenment and Emancipation, there has been a tug-of-war within us all. Once granted the ability to live beyond parochial communal boundaries, we seized the opportunity to do so. With permeable communal walls and with fluid social identities, Jews entered into new personal and professional space, relishing the unprecedented freedoms of citizens of the modern world. And because here in America the internal and external forces that compelled us to remain tightly knit were no longer in play, the Jewish community could no longer assume that Jews would "do Jewish with other Jews." The realignment of communal points of association was not, and is not, limited to the Jewish world. As Robert Putnam argued in his aptly titled book *Bowling Alone*, the fabric of all institutions of communal life – PTAs, Rotary clubs, bowling leagues, and the like – has also frayed. The last fifty years of American life have yielded a world of increasing disconnect – from family, from friends, from communal life. And as if these forces weren't enough, our reservoir of social capital has been further depleted in recent years by new technologies that, though seemingly intended to connect people, actually further undermine our ability to create communities of meaning. No longer, writes Howard Gardner in *The App Generation*, must one ask for directions, participate in face-to-face conversation, or engage in dialogue beyond 140 characters. It is a perfect storm of circumstances, from the Emancipation to the iPhone – a world of diminished intimacy between teens, between adults, and between Jews. It is the bitter irony of our moment. Never before has it been as easy to connect to other Jews, never before has the modern Jew been as alienated from his or her Jewish community.

Which is why, by any means necessary, social and actual capital must be directed towards creating communal structures that are aimed to be socially (not theologically) orthodox. Of course we cherish our autonomy, but deep down we want to be at home in our Jewishness; we want to be part of our people. "To be free and to belong," to paraphrase Natan Sharansky, these are the two, sometimes contradictory, impulses within each of us. The strength of this synagogue and others, is that for so many people they serve as the hub of communal and personal identity – at times of joy and sorrow, a place of prayer, learning, and compassion. Synagogues are the only Jewish institutions on the American landscape whose primary mission is to generate the connective tissue that binds one Jew to another and one generation to the next. But to be fair to the conversation, we also need to cheer on those efforts that seek to accomplish the same goal by other means: Jewish camping, Birthright, Jewish day schools, and others. Our attention and support can and should run proudly against the grain of contemporary American life. We must, at every juncture, create opportunities for Jews to do Jewish with other Jews, even when – especially when – the rest of the world would tell us otherwise.

And there is one final element – perhaps the most critical – and that element is you. Far too often, far too many people sit around and kvetch about the movements, that the leaders of Orthodox, Reform, or Conservative Judaism are yet again missing an historic opportunity to reinvigorate Jewish life. We blame some underpaid ideologue or funding-strapped programmer sitting in a midtown office building as if they are responsible for our personal Jewish identity. We need to stop doing this. The only person stopping you from building Jewish identity is you. It is not rocket science. Find a family with kids the same age as yours, call them this week and invite them over for Friday night dinner, and then do it the next week and the week after that. Sign up for a class. When picking your next vacation, choose to go on a synagogue trip to Israel. Designate one night a week (you have seven of them) to "do Jewish with other Jews." Find a Jewish organization committed to your highest values and get involved. Do anything. Just don't sit around bemoaning the state of the organized Jewish world, when you yourself have not organized yourself to step into that very world that you are criticizing so vocally from the bleachers.

Im b'ḥukkotai teilekhu,v'et mitzvotai tishmoru, "If you walk in my laws and observe my commandments," our Torah reading begins, "then you shall be blessed." (Leviticus 26:3) The medieval commentator Rashi remarked on the seeming redundancy of the verse. Wouldn't it have been enough to say only "If you observe my commandments?" What does "walk in my laws" add? Rashi explains that to receive God's blessing, one must be intensively immersed in the Torah of our people. Yes, we must observe the commandments, but equally important is that we should surround ourselves, literally toiling, collectively, in doing Jewish with other Jews.

My Hillel director, mentor, and friend Michael Brooks once told me: we Jews spend so much time drawing lines among ourselves, further subdividing a people that isn't all that big to begin with. Ultimately there is only one line that matters, the line separating who has opted into the Jewish community and who has opted out. Take a leap of faith, be on the right side of the line, immerse yourself and write yourself into the narrative of the greatest story ever told. Most of all, leave the light on, so others know they can do the same.

Check Your Jewish Privilege

Although the expression has been in use for twenty-five years, it was not until two weeks ago that I actually heard the phrase "check your privilege." Coined by social justice activist Peggy McIntosh in a 1988 article called "Unpacking the Invisible Backpack," the expression "check your privilege" refers to the act of acknowledging the advantages and benefits conferred upon you by the fact of your having been born into a particular race, gender, ethnicity, religion, etc. A longtime advocate for women's rights, McIntosh knew the universe of entitlements extended to men, entitlements which, having been denied to exist by those very men, were systemically reinforced. The stir surrounding her article was that McIntosh turned the lens of self-examination on herself, courageously raising the question of race, and the degree to which she carried an "invisible weightless knapsack" of unearned assets and privileges simply by having been born white. The list ranged from the structural to the mundane: the choice of what neighborhood to live in, the comfort of having never been racially profiled, and the ease of being able to find dolls, toys and greeting cards featuring people of her own race. In "checking her privilege" as a white woman, McIntosh identified for herself and the rest of the world the earned and unearned advantages conferred on her and denied to people of color, a small but altogether necessary first step towards addressing the systemic inequalities of our society.

But it was not until two weeks ago that the conversation about checking one's privilege turned to the Jewish community. Tal Fortgang, a Princeton University freshman, wrote a piece on the subject in the Princeton *Tory*, soon republished to a wider readership in *Time* magazine. As a white Jewish male on a college campus, Fortgang had been told on several occasions to "check his privilege," lest he forget that the benefits he enjoys in his advantaged existence are neither earned, nor shared by all, but rather byproducts of his fortuitous birth. Responding to such claims, Fortgang unleashed a torrent of his family's historical narrative, objecting to the insinuation that his station in life had come easy. "Perhaps," he begins, "it's the privilege my grandfather and his brother had to flee their home as teenagers when the Nazis invaded Poland, leaving their mother and five younger siblings behind, running and running until they reached a DP camp in Siberia, where they would do years of hard labor in the bitter cold until WWII ended." "Or maybe," Fortgang writes, "it's the privilege my grandmother had of spending weeks upon weeks on a death march through Polish forests in subzero temperatures . . ." "Perhaps," he continues, "it was the privilege my great-grandmother and those five great-aunts and uncles I never knew had of being shot into an open grave outside their hometown. Maybe that's my privilege." How dare they? Those people, Fortgang rages, demand that I check my privilege, not knowing my past. Fortgang concludes his piece with a strident air, "I have checked my privilege. And I apologize for nothing."

As important as it is to read Fortgang, I also urge you to read the response written by Samuel Freedman in last week's *Forward*. Freedman explains that Fortgang, in drawing on his family's past sufferings in the Shoah, has overlooked the incredibly blessed and fortuitous circumstances of his own existence. ". . . If you are able to live in New Rochelle, New York, and if you are able to attend the SAR Academy Day School, both of which Fortgang has done, and if just maybe you also had tutoring or test-prep classes, and at the least had the proximate example of college-educated parents, none of that means you did not toil; it just meant that you started your toil with assets not available to the children of less prosperous, less educated families." "As a college freshman," Freedman explains, "Fortgang necessarily lacks the perspective to see that his family's history, indeed Jewish history, is a saga of both persecution and achievement, of being both underdog and overdog . . . He does not seem to accept the existence of inherited advantage."

The storm prompted by the dueling articles was undoubtedly not due to any one individual or college campus. Rather, the exchange touched on a much bigger and much more sensitive nerve about the contemporary Jewish condition – Jewish power, Jewish persecution, and our uneasy efforts to balance the reality of the two. Such a small people, so much hurt, and yet so many Nobel prizes. A people despised and dispersed; a full third of us exterminated a mere seventy years ago. And yet, look around you: we aren't doing so bad. A quarter of the world's population, according to ADL statistics released this month, is anti-Semitic. The threat is present and real and the shootings in Brussels this past week only remind us of this fact. And yet, never before, by any metric, have the Jewish people been as secure, safe, and frankly, powerful as we are now. No, it was not always this way, but to be born Jewish today is to be born into the most privileged circumstances. Certainly, if you, like me, are under fifty, then you arrived in this world as a Jew with advantages that are yours to enjoy but not entirely of your own making. It is a disorienting set of circumstances, we are not exactly sure what to do about it, and so it is understandable if we are a bit sensitive when it is discussed publicly.

It is a circumstance, incidentally, that is not entirely without precedent. One need look no further than the protagonist of this week's haftarah, Samson, to encounter a man whose privileged stature was pre-ordained, literally, in utero. An angel of the Lord appeared to Samson's mother: ". . . you shall conceive and bear a son ... the boy is to be a Nazirite to God from the womb on. He shall be the first to deliver Israel from the Philistines." (Judges 13:5) This would not be the last Jewish boy to arrive in this world to a Jewish mother believing him to be the center, if not the savior, of the universe. And while the presence of my wife and son dictate that I choose my next few words carefully, we do not need a degree in psychology to telescope the consequences of being raised by a smothering Jewish mother with such an inflated estimation of her offspring. The coddling and hand-holding, leading to privilege, leading to entitlement, and yes – because we know how Samson's story will turn out – eventually to an abdication of purpose. The tragedy of Samson isn't merely that he grew up to be a slothful, weak-willed, Philistine womanizer. The tragedy of Samson is that he came into this world to fulfill an explicit purpose in the arc of Jewish history. He had the tools, he had the strength, he had the gifts; and then he fell short. He failed to check the privilege of his existence and thus failed to fulfill the very reason for his being. As numerous scholars have pointed out, the tale of Samson is not just the story of a single man, or a morality tale with universal application. Samson is Israel personified; his failure represents the failed opportunity of Israel to assess its circumstances and fulfill its generational obligations.

It is a story that hits uncomfortably close to home for our generation. The more I thought about the Fortgang-Freedman exchange, the more I came to believe that they failed to raise the question that actually matters. The invocation of one's past suffering, important as it may be, is entirely secondary to the question of one's present and future. In a world of privilege, it doesn't really matter whether you arrived at that station by way of persecution or not. What ultimately matters is, what are you going to do with that privilege today? If you are Jewish and alive right now, then you are living in the best one percent of one percent of all of Jewish history. The comfort, the security, the resources, the State of Israel – it has never been so good. My fear, however, is that we – like Samson – are so coddled by our circumstances that we are missing the historic window of opportunity in which we live. We turn our energies and our hearts away from our people, believing that because there is no existential crisis, our attention and contributions are not needed. We tell ourselves that the Jewish world can live without us, our engagement, and our support. This is wrong! As my high school cross-country coach once screamed at me: "Cosgrove, races are won and lost on the downhills!" It is precisely because of our circumstances that we must be alert to the needs of the hour. We have a purpose to play in the arc of Jewish history. It is precisely at moments like this that we must plan for the Jewish future, building the institutions and identities that will hold us in strength. This is the litmus test of our people. Sure we have our share of self-made men, but the heroes of our people – Joseph, Moses, and Queen Esther – are those individuals who came to understand that it was precisely because of their privilege, precisely because the easy, purposeless life was theirs if they wanted it, that they must choose otherwise. They are our heroes because despite their station in life, or more precisely, because of their station in life, they threw their lot in with our people, making the contributions for which future generations remain eternally grateful.

Akavyah Ben Mahalel taught: "Reflect upon three things and you will not come to commit sin. Know from where you came, to where you are going, and before whom you will be called on to give an account and reckoning." (*Pirkei Avot* 3:1) All living things have a common and modest origin. No matter who we are – rich or poor, privileged or persecuted – we all have a single fate. These are the equalizers shared by every one of us. But some of us, and I would dare say, all of us in this room, have been born into circumstances about which past generations could have only dreamed. So yes, check your privilege. Live with an awareness that you have been afforded opportunities and gifts enjoyed neither by your predecessors nor by most of humanity today. Let the feeling sink in, be grateful for it, there is no shame in it; you can even enjoy it. And now ask the next question, the one that really matters. In the words of the Psalmist: "How can I repay the Lord for this bounty bestowed unto me?" (116:12) Leverage the question, let it inspire you, and most importantly, let it motivate you do something fantastic towards the betterment of our people.

Shavuot

What We Talk About When We Talk About Conversion

In retrospect, Shavuot would have been a far more sensible time to deliver a sermon on the subject of conversion. "Wherever you go, I will go; wherever you lodge, I will lodge. Your people shall be my people, and your God my God." (Ruth 1:16) These words spoken by Ruth to her mother-in-law Naomi are not just the slogan of today's festival, but the anthem for all such righteous converts. Just as the Jewish people entered the covenant with God at Mount Sinai, so too Ruth joined our people, and through today, all men and women seeking to bind their destiny to the destiny of the Jewish people turn to the Shavuot hero Ruth as the paradigm for their journey. If there is a time begging for a Rabbi to talk about conversion, Shavuot is the obvious choice.

As you may recall, I chose otherwise. On a quiet Shabbat in February of last year, I floated a trial balloon regarding our approach to conversion. What if, I suggested, we modify the present policy – whereby a would-be Jew enters a year-long course of study and practice that culminates in conversion – to a model in which a person converts first and then learns what being a Jew is all about? Citing the Talmudic precedent of Hillel and the imperfect analogy of joining a gym, I advocated that such an approach serves to lower the barriers of entry faced by prospective Jews. I suggested then, and affirm today, that it is a policy that is muscular in both its stringencies and leniencies. It affirms, without apologies, the value of marrying a Jew and creating a Jewish home, but does so in a way that welcomes the would-be

Jew instantly and warmly. I said then, and affirm today, that I am in the business of creating Jewish homes. Like many congregational rabbis, I am approached regularly by interfaith couples on the cusp of settling down; many of them, incidentally, are children of our congregation. Understanding, as I do, the role of a rabbi to be an agent for the creation of Jewish homes, I see such a policy change as a step in the right direction towards easing the process of joining our people. The intent was explicit and clear, the legal arguments surmountable, the Orthodox don't accept our conversions anyway, and the potential boon to our people – immeasurable.

Nearly a year and a half later, I can share that whatever the strengths and weaknesses of the proposal may be, the most interesting part has been the reaction it received. An idea that was, in all honesty, prompted by the day-to-day life of a congregational rabbi struck a nerve well beyond the walls of this synagogue. Since delivering the sermon, I have been asked to present the idea in communal settings, academic contexts, outreach think tanks, and conference plenaries. From an editorial in *The Jewish Week* the week following the sermon, through an editorial in this week's *Forward*, the idea continues to be discussed. I have received public and private feedback ranging from the most scathing to the most supportive – with many telling me that my proposal does not go far or fast enough. All this, mind you, without a single policy change: one talk that has led to a whole lot of talk.

So why the stir? Why the fuss? Why did the idea strike a nerve? My first answer has to do with what was, from a publicity standpoint, fortuitous timing. Last year's publication of the Pew study of American Jewry and UJA-Federation's study of New York Jewry provided the hard analysis to back up what we all know to be the anecdotal narrative of our community and our own families. The fluid social boundaries, the slackening of affiliation, the rising rates of late-marriage, non-marriage, and intermarriage, the decline in fertility rates – all impacting our present and future numbers. A new approach to conversion is a rather elegant response to a fairly straightforward math problem. If, as the Pew study indicates, about seventy percent of non-Orthodox Jews are likely to marry non-Jews; and if, as the Pew study indicates, less than two percent of American Jews are Jews by Choice; and if studies indicate there is an exponentially greater chance of raising Jewish children when both parents identify as Jewish; and if you think having more Jews in the world is a good thing; then why wouldn't you adopt such a policy on conversion? As the *Forward* editorial reports, ". . . in 1950 there was one Mormon for every 10 Jews. Now there are more Mormons in the world than Jews . . ." The divergent demographic narratives have nothing to do with the merits of one faith over the other, but rather the willingness of Mormons and reticence of Jews to deploy mechanisms welcoming converts. Barring excluding ourselves from secular culture, universities, and otherwise, my children and yours will, in all likelihood, sit in freshman English next to a cute non-Jewish boy or girl with whom there exists a statistical chance that they will fall in love. So while I have no policy recommendations to lessen the likelihood of that occurrence, what I can suggest is a communal posture aimed at making their potential future home a Jewish one.

But the second, and frankly, far more substantive reason I believe the sermon caused a fuss was because when Jews talk about conversion, we are actually talking about something different and deeper: we are talking about the Jewish condition and the condition of Judaism. Conversion is a window into our souls, who we are, and our self-perception. We tell ourselves we are talking about mundane procedural steps by which a gentile can convert to Judaism, but it is really not about that person. It is about me, it is about you, it is about all of us.

Let me explain.

As I have thrown myself into the legal and historical literature regarding conversion, I have become more and more intrigued by the diversity of views embedded in Jewish sources regarding the would-be Jew. A few examples. Tractate Gerim in the Babylonian Talmud begins famously: "Cherished are the converts. For everywhere Scripture speaks of them in the same terms as it does Israel." (4:2-4) Elsewhere, however, Tosafot in Tractate Kiddushin (70b) claims, "Converts are problematic," literally like a scab. Further back, in biblical texts, there is the story of Dinah, a rather gruesome narrative reflecting deep suspicion of the non-Israelite seeking to join the tribe. On the other hand, the flowing poetry of Isaiah 56 describes a God who embraces all those who attach themselves to the Lord. The book of Ruth, as mentioned, represents a posture of acceptance; King David himself is a descendant of Ruth. And yet, as my teacher Dr. Ziony Zevit has suggested, the dating of the book of Ruth to the Persian exile may be a counterbalance to the book of Ezra, who commanded all the returning exiles to divorce their foreign wives. And let's not forget Hillel and Shammai: Shammai who beat the prospective convert away with a stick, and Hillel who received him with a full embrace.

Each of these texts, and there are many others, represents a different attitude towards conversion. Most emerge out of different contexts, but some, like Hillel and Shammai, reflect varied attitudes in the same context. The interesting question is why they thought what they did. Why would someone reject a convert? It could be, perhaps, because there existed a tribal or racial conception of identity – that Jewishness is not merely a religious faith into which one can convert. It could be because in certain slices of Jewish history, Jews were understandably wary of ulterior motives – the emergence of a fifth column from within the ranks – or because of a visceral fear or hatred of "the goyim." Or it could be, as my teacher Dr. David Kraemer recently taught, that Jews feared that the convert would be more scrupulous and exacting in their observance than a born Jew, making the Jewish community self-conscious over any actual or perceived lapses in practice.

It could be a lot of things, and ultimately we do not and may never know what prompted each thinker's opinion. Maybe it has to do with their understanding of Jewish identity, maybe it has to do with Jewish/non-Jewish relations in a particular context, maybe it has to do with how strong or weak the minority Jewish culture perceived themselves to be vis-à-vis the majority non-Jewish culture at a particular moment. I don't know. What I do know is that if conversion is an act of crossing the boundary into the Jewish community, then it necessarily calls on us to define where that boundary is, how it is constituted, and how it can be transcended. Conversion forces us to differentiate between "us" and "them." To put it another way, if we allow ourselves to ask how one of "them" can become one of "us," then at some point we need to ask what exactly is "us." And that, my friends, in this day and age, is an altogether raw and prickly question.

We are not living in the time of the Bible, the Talmud, or Tosafot but in twenty-first-century America, an era of profound generational transition. There are those in this room who were raised, understandably so, with a deep suspicion of the other. After all, it was not so long ago that "the goyim" were trying to exclude us, harm us, or – in the case of the Shoah – kill us. But today, the children and grandchildren of those very people are growing up in an America where being Jewish is neither a stigma, nor necessarily even a point of difference worthy of shaping marital choices. The hovering presence of an Eastern European grandparent differentiating "us" from "them" is increasingly distant, and more of "us" than not have one of "them" in our very families – what Robert Putnam calls the "Aunt Susan Effect" – a beautiful, loving, non-Jewish aunt, uncle, or in-law who is part of our Jewish family.

And so we squirm. In identifying the Aunt Susans, the "Jews of no religion" and all the other new categories of contemporary Jewish identity, we are slowly and uncomfortably waking up to the fact that we no longer live in the world of our fathers. Somewhere in our minds we retain a regnant sense that we should resist the convert, refuse them three times, demand they be better Jews than we are, and erect barriers preventing them from entering our ranks. And even when they do convert, some still ask, "Are they really Jewish?" I get it. In fact, not only do I get it, but I was raised on these assumptions and trained to think accordingly. But it makes no sense. It makes no sense to tell a kid who was born and bar-mitzvahed in a Reform synagogue in Scarsdale, who grew up thinking and feeling he is Jewish, that – because his mother was not Jewish – he must enter a formal conversion program. It makes no sense to throw a roadblock in front of a couple who has taken the time and energy to make an appointment with me to ask how I can facilitate their creating their Jewish home. It makes no sense to try to suss out some nefarious ulterior motive of a prospective convert as if we are living in the Middle Ages. I didn't choose to live as a Jew in this time and place, but I do and so do you. If this is the window we have been granted to strengthen our people, then our policies and postures need to reflect that. Attitudes to conversion, like everything in life, are contextually bound. We must be eyes-wide-open to our present context, and more importantly, capable of formulating policies to address present needs and aspirations.

What we need to do is to do what makes sense for now – not for some long past yesteryear, but for today and tomorrow. Please God, it should be a quiet summer. I intend to spend some of that summer in the library doing research. I will look at the conversion issue from all sides: historical, halachic, sociological, and pastoral. I want to talk to people who have converted to Judaism and to people who are on their way to doing so, along with colleagues and stakeholders who have something to contribute to the conversation. And then I am going to write, to outline a position, and make a recommendation this fall. Not a trial balloon, not a talk, but a policy. First for our congregation, and then for anyone else interested in listening. As with everything we do, the driving question will be "what is best for the Jewish future?" Will it make our people stronger, more numerous, and more engaged? Will we, by virtue of the policy decisions we adopt, emerge with a brighter Jewish future? I look forward to the work ahead. I look forward to our discussions and most of all, I look forward to our congregation taking a leadership role in this conversation.

Two Leaders in One

O ne of my great regrets of my years in Chicago is that I never took a class with Dr. Benjamin Sommer. When I was a doctoral student at the University of Chicago, Dr. Sommer was a professor of Bible on the other side of town at Northwestern University. Though I will always be grateful for his warmth and wise counsel, by the time I might have taken a class with him, he was already on his way to a prestigious appointment as Professor of Bible at the Jewish Theological Seminary. He is, without a doubt, one of the finest scholars of the Hebrew Bible today, his many books and articles blending rigorous scholarship with deep devotion to the Torah. More than once, I have flipped through the JTS course catalogue wishing that I could audit his class, and the welcome mat is always out for him here at Park Avenue. He is a superb teacher. Should you ever have an opportunity to study with him, do yourself a favor and sign up. I promise you, you won't be disappointed.

This morning I want to teach from one of Dr. Sommer's articles, whose subject matter comes directly from this week's parashah. The article was published in the *Journal of Biblical Literature* (Winter 1999: pp. 601–624). Though its title, "Reflecting on Moses: The Redaction of Numbers 11," may not sound like a nail-biter, if I do my job right over the next few minutes, not only will you find the questions Dr. Sommer raises intriguing in their own right, but you will discover as I did that his inquiries have application well beyond the text of the Torah itself.

In a nutshell: In reading our parashah, specifically Numbers, chapters 11-12, Dr. Sommer observes a number of incongruities in the storyline regarding the figure of Moses. There is an unevenness to the text, multiple – almost competing – narrative elements, which for our purposes we will call story A and story B. Just as there are two different creation stories in Genesis 1 and 2, and just as there are multiple versions of Noah and the flood – sometimes with two of each kind of animal on the ark, sometimes with seven – here, too, there seem to be two different narrative strands woven together. Sommer observes the composite nature of the text, and spends the bulk of his article untangling which part is which and how it all fits together.

In story A, Moses is not portrayed in a particularly positive light. When the Israelites complain that they are hungry, Moses erupts into a long and angry outburst, haranguing God for having put him in such a horrible leadership position. "Am I responsible for this people? Moses demands. "Should I have to care for it as if I were its nursing father?" Moses is petulant and bitter and full of self-pity. Worse, Sommer continues, Moses seems to doubt whether God can supply enough food for the Israelites, a lack of trust to which God responds in anger.

Interwoven with that story, however, is another story. As in story A, the people complain, are punished by God, and turn to Moses to assuage God's wrath. Here in story B, however, God appoints seventy elders to assist Moses – affirming Moses' pre-eminent status while helping him spread the burden of leadership he faces. Two men, Eldad and Medad, begin to prophesy in the Israelite camp. Joshua, Moses' right-hand man, fears a challenge to Moses' authority and informs Moses of what he perceives as their rebellion. But it is not Eldad and Medad who receive a rebuke, rather Joshua, to whom Moses expresses his wish "that all the people were prophets." In other words, Moses seems to want others to step up as leaders. No sooner has this crisis passed, than Moses' own siblings, Aaron and Miriam, speak out against their brother, challenging whether indeed God has spoken only through Moses. Not only does the text go to great lengths to signal Moses' humility, "more humble than any other man on earth," but it is Moses himself who prays on behalf of Miriam when she is punished by God for her disloyalty to her brother.

I am not able to cover Sommer's entire article, but the upshot is that embedded in a single narrative there may in fact be two distinct stories that have been spliced together. The Moses A story paints a portrait of a rather self-centered leader, hierarchical, full of first-person declarations and righteous indignation. The other story paints a totally different picture of our leader. Moses B is democratically inclined, self-effacing, and selfless. Sommers lays it out like a grid verse by verse – one Moses, split into two.

All of which leads to the interesting question: why? Why would a single text contain such radically different viewpoints? Is it possible that the author of the Bible, what Bible scholars call "The Redactor," was not aware of the disjointed text? How is it possible that these two mutually exclusive portraits of Moses could be contained in one chapter? Did the author, Sommer asks, suffer from aphasia, or "blindly paste together random scraps in a darkened room?" Is it two narratives, or is it one? What are we to make of these incongruous, if not incompatible, characterizations of our greatest prophet?

To which Sommer answers: "Exactly!" Whether you believe the author or redactor of the Torah to be human or divine, the very point of the uneven text is to reflect the tensions embedded in Moses himself. Was Moses' leadership style hierarchical, personality-driven, and controlling; or was Moses a humble, "not about me," non-hierarchical sort of leader? Was he Moses A or was he Moses B? The question itself is the answer. Moses was Moses A; Moses was Moses B. To paraphrase Faye Dunaway in *Chinatown*: he was Moses A *and* Moses B, and that is the very point the text is trying to communicate.

It is tempting to characterize our greatest leader as exemplifying only one leadership style. But the impossibility of doing that does not stem only from today's Torah reading. The tension exists in his personality from the wicker basket on the Nile right up to Moses' death. There is the Moses of the Burning Bush, resisting the call to leadership, humble and demurring. And there is the assertive Moses, the one who kills the Egyptian, who smashes the tablets, and strikes the rock. Depending on who you are, the text you are citing, and the point you are trying to make, you may be inclined to draw from one model and the ignore the other, but the truth is that they exist side-by-side. At one juncture Moses wishes the people destroyed, and moments later he intercedes on their behalf to stay God's wrath. In one text, Moses stands toe-to-toe with Pharaoh, in another he is but one voice singing among the chorus of Israel as they cross the sea together. Here Moses is identified as the only one to liaise with God, elsewhere he appoints leaders to share the burdens of leadership. "Never again," our Torah will conclude, "did a prophet like Moses arise in Israel." (Deuteronomy 34:10) Which Moses was it? The "it's not about me" Moses, or the "it's all about me" Moses? The answer is that it is a bit of both.

While we have now extended well beyond the scope of Sommer's article, the astute reader of the biblical text knows not only that Moses' leadership style was multidimensional, but that both aspects were necessary for Israel's journey through desert. Were it not for Moses' "just do it" wiring, were it not for his single-mindedness of purpose, the children of Israel would still be languishing in Egypt. And yet, no matter how driven Moses may have been, it is the constancy of his humility that assures both Israel (and the reader) that his actions are never about him. His purpose is always to serve the greater good and fulfill the task at hand. Neither Moses A nor Moses B would have sufficed; both were necessary to lead the Children of Israel from Egypt to the Promised Land.

Ultimately, we also know that neither Moses A, nor Moses B, nor Moses A *and* B was enough. As we shall discover in the weeks to come, there is a direct correlation between the tensions within Moses' leadership style and Israel's readiness to enter a new chapter of their existence. The generation of the desert died in the desert because they were neither able to detach themselves from their past Egyptian servitude, nor did they demonstrate the fortitude of spirit to conquer the land. We can blame the Israelites, but it was arguably the fault of their leader, who failed to create a culture of stewardship that would have empowered them to arrive at their wished for goal. Rarely do we pause to reflect on the fact that the greatest leader in Jewish history – tasked to lead a people into the Promised Land – actually fell short of his stated mission. Yes, he led them through the sea and brought them to the border, but neither he nor the generation of the Exodus would enter the Land. Moses may have been the greatest leader our people has ever known, but anyone studying his leadership style knows that we have as much to learn from his missteps and mistakes as we do from his virtues and victories.

The journeys of our lives can last four years or forty years. Personal, professional, and otherwise, there is not one of us in this room that is not trying to reach a Promised Land. The institutions we are seeking to build – be it our home, our synagogue, or our workplace – call on us to draw on a variety of leadership styles. It is never one or another. Perhaps true wisdom is the ability to know what muscle group to deploy at what moment. And nobody gets it right all the time, not even Moses. We are all works in progress. But maybe, just maybe, if we all walk this world aware of the question, aware of the tension – we will succeed in reaching the banks of the Jordan and some of us, perhaps, may even be lucky enough to enter the Promised Land.

Sh'laḥ L'kha

The Will to Believe

Considering the events that followed his medical school graduation in 1869, it was neither evident nor imaginable that the career of William James would turn out the way it did. One of, if not the most, important intellectuals of nineteenth-century America, William James founded the philosophical school of Pragmatism. His lectures, essays, and books, blending psychology, philosophy, and theology continue to shape American discourse to this day. Having been introduced to his writings at a critical stage of my own religious and intellectual development, I am acutely aware of the ongoing role he has in influencing my thinking on matters of God, faith, and, frankly, pretty much everything else.

But when James graduated from medical school, his bright future was anything but certain. As a young man he had suffered from a variety of ailments. After he entered medical school, his condition grew progressively worse, as he fought eyestrain, back problems, and bouts of suicidal depression. A bad situation turned worse when, upon being awarded his MD from Harvard in 1869, James experienced a total collapse and breakdown. Louis Menand describes his diary from this period as "a record of misery and self-loathing." (*Metaphysical Club*, p. 218) For the next three years, James lived at home facing a "crisis of meaning." His breakthrough and eventual recovery came by way of reading an essay by the French philosopher Charles Renouvier, which, in a nutshell, affirmed the role of free will in human psychology. Having been granted the gift of choice, as human beings we must choose. Not only are we empowered, but we are obligated to take the initiative to determine the circumstances of our existence. Neither James' depression nor the psychosomatic disorders that incapacitated him would disappear overnight, but from that moment on, James understood the critical role his personal resolve played in addressing his melancholy existence. To put it plainly, he admitted that it was up to him to bring himself out of his funk. Despite the fact that life is filled with daunting unknowns, the hovering "mights," "maybes," and "what ifs" of existence that can immobilize even the most resilient soul, James realized that it was in his power to choose to alter his psychological state. In his own words, "My first act of free will shall be to believe in free will."

Not surprisingly, there is a direct line that can be traced from his personal recuperation to the philosophy he would write in the decades to come. The title of his most famous collection of essays, *The Will to Believe*, says it all. "Believe that life is worth living," James wrote, "and your belief will help create the fact." Pessimism, James explains, is a religious disease. Our social and biological circumstances may or may not be in our control, but our "will to believe" – in God, in ourselves, and in the future – most assuredly is.

The failings of the Israelites in this week's Torah reading are as numerous as they are varied, but at the root of it all, I believe, is the toxic and self-defeating sentiment of pessimism that James understood to exist at every stalled or stillborn life journey. The trip to the Promised Land was not intended to last forty years. Like going to Wisconsin, the plan was to zip into the desert, pick up the Ten Commandments, and zip right out again. But as we know from the Torah readings of these weeks, very little ends up going according to plan. Last week, the rumblings began with a challenge to Moses' leadership and then the bitter murmurings of Israelites. "We remember the fish that we used to eat free in Egypt," they cried, "the cucumbers, the leeks, the onions, and the garlic." Succumbing to the tricks of memory, the Israelites somehow elide and smooth over the pain and horror of their past enslavement. An insidious and destabilizing disquiet starts to spread through the people.

The bottom falls out in this week's parashah. Twelve spies are sent to scout out the land. Find out, Moses asks, if the country is good or bad. Are the towns open or fortified? Is the soil rich or poor? For forty days they scouted the land, and ten of the spies returned with a gloom-filled report. "We cannot attack that people, for it is stronger than we . . . The country that we traversed and scouted is one that devours it settlers." (Numbers 13:31-32) In the midst of the mutinous calumny, Joshua and Caleb counter, "Let us by all means go up, and we shall gain possession of it." But by then it was too late. The sin of the spies was not that they lied; nobody ever said this was going to be easy. Their sin, rather, was their pessimism; that having been appointed to a leadership position, they responded with a crisis of confidence. "We looked like grasshoppers to ourselves, and so we must have looked to them." This is the essence of their failure, that they were so convinced of their own inadequacies – the "mights," "maybes," and "what ifs" of their uncertain moment – that they froze up. They were asked *how* to conquer the land, not *if* it should be conquered. The outcome was actually already foretold; they just needed to execute the plan. But they couldn't. As Professor Adriane Leveen explains, it is precisely because the memories of their Egyptian past had colonized their present that they failed to grab hold of their future. (*Memory and Tradition*, p. 84). As they were mired in their past, their loss of resolve obfuscated their vision forward, and whatever momentum they had was for naught.

The hammer comes down and their fate is sealed. Forty years of wilderness wandering corresponding to the forty-day scouting mission. Having failed to demonstrate faith in God, faith in the future, faith in themselves, the Exodus generation sealed their fate. Their destiny was to die in the desert. The saddest part is that it was all avoidable. They could have opted to be bold, to be courageous, and to press forward with hope. But they didn't; they chose otherwise. Their misguided and corrosive sentimentality for the past, their despondency regarding their present, all leading to a perceived loss of free will regarding their future. The problem was not insurmountable obstacles; the task was altogether doable. The problem was that Israel lacked the spiritual pugilism the moment called for. It is no wonder they lost the fight.

Ever since the generation of the desert, it is by way of their missteps that we measure our own journeys. By any metric, this year coming to a close has been a difficult one for our people. The news on the home front has not been good. The emergent narrative is of an uninspired and disengaged American Jewish community – flagging numbers, apathetic Jews, and unresponsive, tone-deaf institutions. The data has led to a lot of head scratching, a fair amount of finger pointing, and an all-consuming mood of doom and gloom. And the news from Israel is not any better. A Jewish year that began with announcements of peace initiatives has devolved into a vicious cycle of posturing, recriminations, and unilateral assertions of power – all of which seems to be leading to a renewed cycle of violence. Most sad, as I have said on more than one occasion, is the fraying of the bonds between the two centers of world Jewry. A small people whose historic strength comes from a feeling of *arevut* – Jews being responsible one for another – is now being subdivided into left and right, here and there, secular and religious. Like a person given the diagnosis of a chronic condition, the Jewish people faces more "mights, "maybes," and "what ifs" than we know what to do with. It is all very overwhelming. Not surprisingly, there are those who seek to turn back and return to the days of old, trying to recapture glory days that never actually existed. There are those who respond in anger, who, in the face of uncertainty, are angry with God and each other. And there are those who, given the odds, have lost the will to press forward. They sit nervously on the sidelines waiting for the storm to pass. "What can I do?" they mutter. The fight has long left their soul. None of us need look far to see such people. Their negativity is around us, not so different from the mood of the failed desert generation.

To which I say to you today: Not me, not us; not here, not ever.

The late Maya Angelou reminded us that "Courage is the most important of all the virtues, because without courage you can't practice any other virtue consistently." As a people, our faith is directed not just towards God or each other. Our faith is a combination of courage and hope wrought from within that impels us to work feverishly towards a bright Jewish future. Long before William James, as Jews we understood that the choice between life and death is always before us, and we always "choose life." It is not that we are unaware of the hurdles we face or the possibility of failure. If anything, we demand that our eyes be wide open to the challenges and we be as vigilant and responsive to the landscape as humanly possible. But it is because we know that each one of us is the author of a narrative yet to be written, that we also know that the possibility of hope exists. This belief in the hope of possibility and the possibility of hope is not just the essence of courage, not just the essence of faith, but the essence of our people. For two thousand years and change, as long as a Jewish soul yearns, our hope, *tik-*

vah, is never lost. Yes, the problems are daunting; yes, the future is uncertain; and no, I don't have all the answers. But that's the way it's always been, and our challenges must be seen equally as opportunities. As Shakespeare wrote, "Sweet are the uses of adversity." Our mood must be one of creativity and collaboration, and most of all, courage. We must be pugilists of the spirit. That will be the difference between success and failure.

The story is told of a rabbi who asked his students to name the greatest moment of Jewish history. The students argued amongst themselves – one insisting it was the splitting of the sea, another claiming that it was the giving of Torah at Mount Sinai. Upon hearing all their answers, the rabbi let the room settle down and quietly responded, "No, the greatest moment in Jewish history is right now."

This answer is the one and only response that we dare articulate. We must be, as Heschel once wrote, "optimists against our better judgment." We have free will, we have the choice, and no matter how hard, we must always find some reason to believe. Our appreciation for the Jewish past need not interfere with our obligations to the Jewish future. The path forward is anything but certain, and unlike the desert journey of the Israelites of old, neither its duration nor its destination is altogether clear. But our moment has blessings and opportunities about which past generations could only dream. It is incumbent upon us to identify these gifts and leverage them towards the future. After all, it was for us that past generations toiled, and so too, it is the generations to come whom we serve today.

William James concluded his most famous essay, "The Will to Believe," with these words: "We stand on a mountain pass in the midst of whirling snow and blinding mist, through which we get glimpses now and then of paths which may be deceptive. If we stand still we shall be frozen to death. If we take the wrong road we may be dashed to pieces. We do not certainly know whether there is any right one. What must we do? 'Be strong, and of good courage.' Act for the best, hope for the best, and take what comes. If death ends all, we cannot meet death better."

I am not sure how well James knew his Bible, but with all due to respect, we said the same thing a whole lot earlier and a bit better. *Luleh he'emanti lirot b'tuv Adonai b'eretz ḥayim. Kaveh el Adonai, ḥazak v'ya'ametz libekha v'kaveh el Adonai.* "Mine is the faith that I shall surely see the Lord's goodness in the land of the living. Hope in the Lord and be strong. Take courage, hope in the Lord!" (Psalm 27:13-14) Or earlier and better yet, what Caleb and Joshua said: *Aloh na'aleh v'rashnu otah, ki yakhol nukhal lah,* "Let us by all means go up, and we shall gain possession of it. We are well able to do it." (Numbers 13:30)

The choice is ours. Let us choose to greet our future with courage, and in doing so, step boldly towards the Promised Land.

Park Avenue Synagogue

Park Avenue Synagogue – *Agudat Yesharim,* the Association of the Righteous – was founded in 1882. From modest beginnings, it has grown into the flagship congregation of the Conservative movement. In 1882 a group of German-speaking Jews founded a congregation and named it Temple Gates of Hope. They converted a church building at 115 East 86th Street into a synagogue and soon the new congregation was known as the Eighty-Sixth Street Temple. Some twelve years after its founding, the synagogue joined together with Congregation Agudat Yesharim, which gave the congregation its Hebrew name, which appears on the cornerstone of the Rita and George M. Shapiro House at the corner of Madison Avenue and 87th Street. In this congregation the sermons were still preached in German. More amalgamations were to come. A nearby synagogue, the Seventy-Second Street Temple – itself a product of the earlier merger of Beth Israel and Bikkur Cholim, two congregations that had their beginnings on the Lower East Side in the 1840s and moved uptown to Lexington Avenue and 72nd Street in 1920 – merged with the Eighty-Sixth Street Temple/Agudat Yesharim.

In 1923 the Eighty-Sixth Street Temple petitioned the State of New York to change its name to Park Avenue Synagogue. A new sanctuary was constructed on 87th Street three years later and dedicated in March 1927. This building remains the present-day sanctuary. In 1928 the last of the mergers took place when Atereth Israel, a congregation of Alsatian Jews who worshipped in their building on East 82nd Street, added their strength to the Park Avenue Synagogue.

Designed by architect Walter Schneider in 1926, the synagogue building is one of the last synagogues to have been built in the Moorish style, which first became popular in the 1850s in Europe. It features one of the most beautiful cast stone façades in New York and a hand-painted *bimah*. Moorish decoration is used throughout the interior of the sanctuary, from Arabesque dadoes to the design for the domed ceiling.

In 1954 a new building was dedicated in memory of Rabbi Milton Steinberg, who had come to the Park Avenue Synagogue in 1933. It was designed by Kelly and Gruzen with architect Robert Greenstein (a Park Avenue Synagogue congregant and former student of Le Corbusier). The renowned American artist Adolph Gottlieb was commissioned to design its stained glass curtain wall façade, the largest continuous expanse of stained glass of its time. Gottlieb's images were intended to reflect Rabbi Steinberg's teachings, which advocated the integration of traditional Jewish practice within modernity and American experience.

In 1980 this building was incorporated into the Rita and George M. Shapiro House, housing the educational facilities of the synagogue. It features a distinctive rusticated façade of Mankato limestone, the color of Jerusalem stone when fully matured, and was designed by Bassuk Panero & Zelnick architects and modified by Schuman, Lichenstein, Calman & Efron with the assistance of James Rush Jarrett and Dean Bernard Spring of the School of Architecture at City University.

Prominently displayed on its façade are two bronze sculptures by Nathan Rapoport, "Tragedy and Triumph." The lower bas relief depicts Dr. Janusz Korczak surrounded by the children of his orphanage in Warsaw as they were deported to their death at Treblinka. The upper panel depicts three Israelis – a pioneer, a soldier, and an older man – carrying back to Israel the Menorah that was removed from the Temple by Titus and the Romans during the destruction of Jerusalem. The inscribed dedication reads: "To the sacred memory of the million Jewish children who perished in the Holocaust." Above the dedication is the Hebrew word *Zakhor* – Remember. Dedicated as a living memorial to the Holocaust, this building expresses Park Avenue Synagogue's hope that the memory of these children will inspire new generations of educated and proud Jews and ensure the continuity of Jewish tradition, history, faith, and heritage.